Forex Trading + Options Trading 2 book in 1

Book 1: Forex Trading
Beginner's Guide to Make Money with *Trading Forex*
Book 2: Options Trading
Advanced Income Strategies for Beginners in Investing Alternative
By: Branden Turner

Table of Contents

Book 1: Forex Trading

Book 2: **Options Trading**

Forex Trading

The Ultimate Beginner's Guide That Shows the Secrets and the Strategies to Make Money with Trading Forex

By: Branden Turner

Introduction

Congratulations on downloading *Forex Trading: The Ultimate Beginner's Guide That Shows the Secrets and the Strategies to Make Money Trading Forex* and thank you for doing so.

The following chapters will discuss every aspect of forex, trading, and investing that you need to know so you can start trading efficiently.

There are plenty of books on this subject on the market, so thanks again for choosing this one! Every effort was made to ensure it is full of as much useful information as possible. Please enjoy!

Chapter 1: Getting Started

In this book, we will show you all the steps you need to take to invest in forex from home. We will show you how to play on the forex market, how to choose the best pairs to invest in, but above all, how to invest in forex and currencies.

In addition, we will also mention the possible methods to invest in online forex markets, thanks to online trading. All the concepts that you will find in this guide have been written to be understood also by people unrelated to the world of online trading and the stock exchange who have decided to inquire to start investing in the stock market.

Investing in the forex market means buying and selling currencies, aiming to earn between the price difference (purchase and sale). In the world of the forex market, as in other major financial markets (for example, the stock market and CFD), you can earn both when there is an increase in the value of a stock and when there is a fall in the value of a stock.

Today, thanks to online trading, it is possible to invest in forex simply from home without problems. This is possible thanks to online trading platforms better known as brokers.

These days, it is possible to invest in the foreign exchange mainly through the following methods:

1. Forex market;
2. Binary options trading; and
3. CFD trading (contract for difference)

In this case, you can choose one of the following online, regulated, and authorized trading platforms and shown below:

1. Markets.com
2. 24option.com

3. iqoption.com
4. BDSwiss.com

In short, with online trading, everyone can start making money on the forex market. It doesn't matter whether you are a novice trader or an experienced trader. Online trading is offered to everyone, thanks to the training offered by its broker, which teaches the basics of trading. Moreover, many brokers today allow you to practice with a demo account, where all traders can test not only the trading platform, but they can also start experimenting with their trading strategies and take their first steps in this fantastic world.

Chapter 2: Trading or Saving?

Very often, the concepts of saving and investing are confused, as well as that of "saver" and "trader". However, there are substantial differences that need to be understood before diving deeper into the subject of money.

In this chapter, we will explain what saving and investing are, analyzing which choice is more convenient today.

Saving means taking out a portion of income received that you deliberately choose not to consume immediately, but to store in a bank account for the future. Saving often results in the tranquillity guaranteed by the availability of resources to deal with unexpected situations.

Savings can then be allocated to investment, and this is the main analogy between the two concepts. The investment may be of the "economic" type (such as the purchase of a car or company machinery) or of the "financial" type (such as the purchase of a security or mutual fund with the objective to see capital growth over time). However, unlike savings, in the case of investing, the achievement of the desired objective is uncertain (for example, a stock may lose value), so the result can be negative, compromising the amounts saved.

Which Is Better?

If the question is whether it's better to save or invest, the answer is probably "both". The choice depends on your financial situation and your personal goals.

Savings can be used to invest, but it can also be used in other ways. In fact, the money saved can also be deposited in the bank to reduce risks (theft). But this, unlike what many people think, is a wrong and unprofitable choice: money tends to lose purchasing power over time due to inflation. In other words, if you save $100 today, you will be able to get less out of that money than today in 20 years. This is why saving money is, often, the wrong choice if you want to get wealthy.

Assuming an average increase in the cost of living around 2% and a saved sum of $5,000, this sum will fall to real $4,500 in 5 years—that is 10% less, excluding banking taxes! Obviously, you can keep the savings at home (under the classic mattress), but with all the risks that come with it.

What Is the Difference Between Trading and Saving?

Let's repeat it once again to get it better: saving means to put money aside little by little to accumulate a certain sum. Usually, you save for a certain goal, like going on vacation, buying a car, or for emergencies that could happen.

On the other hand, trading means taking a part of the money to make it grow, buying tools that can increase its value like currencies, real estates, and ETFs.

Who Should Save?

Obviously, everyone should try to save a part of his/her money. The rule is to have a way on your bank account at least the necessary to "survive" for three months and cover the main expenses (such as food and rent). This will offer air pocket, in case of inconvenient and unexpected situations.

Saving, therefore, is a rule; and as every good rule, it has its exceptions. You can, in fact, stop putting aside the money when:

- you have too much debt and you are trying to pay it off; and
- the family has priority and could not go on in case of unfortunate events to one of its members.

Even when you have set aside enough for emergencies, you do not have to stop saving. The goal of everyone should be to put aside at least 10% of their salary every month, perhaps starting from 5% and gradually scaling up. To make things easier, you can save money by thinking of any objective, like having enough money for a great honeymoon or to get a new car.

Having a goal is essential, so you know what you're saving for. Every reach person has financial goals, so it is a good habit to pick up.

When Is the Time to Trade?

When you save money, you need to have a goal to when and how to trade your savings. In this case, it is important to know what your short-term, medium-term, and long-term goals are.

- With "short-term goals", we mean goals for the next 3 years;
- With "medium-term", those are things planned for the next 3-10 years
- The "long-term goals" are those for which you will not need the money back for at least 10 years or more

For short-term objectives, you usually invest through deposit accounts, which allow you to get a minimum return in a short amount of time. However, this has been a bit shrinking in the last period (deposit rates are at the lowest). For medium-term to long-term objectives, it is instead advisable to invest in the market to avoid the reduction in value that inflation produces on "still" money. The market usually guarantees higher returns than deposit accounts over longer periods, and having a well-constructed portfolio helps a lot in this regard.

For those approaching or exceeding 30 years of age, having medium-term to long-term goals is advisable. Investing and setting aside money for retirement can be a good start.

To sum up the concept, everything depends on your time horizon:

1. If you think about using the money within one or three years, save it.

1. If you do not need this money for the next 10 years, invest it.

If, on the other hand, you plan on using the savings in the next 5 or 10 years, but you want to still have money set aside in your bank account, then you will have to do both. Keep in mind that this is much harder and requires more discipline. However, with the right mindset, it is certainly the best option.

What Does Trading Wisely Mean?

Since the importance of the investment is well-established, it should also be emphasized that there is no recipe to guarantee the success of an investment.

However, following some prudential rules can help minimize risks.

First of all, we need to avoid the dream of making money overnight. On the market, there are professional operators and experts, who dedicate all their time to this activity, but they often make mistakes as well—just to say how difficult it is and how "get rich quick schemes" do not exist.

One strategy that every investor needs to master to reduce the risk is diversification. This means not putting all your eggs in one basket, but spreading your resources on different assets. When the invested amount grows, it becomes more important to diversify not only between the asset classes (stocks, bonds, commodities) but also geographically (taking into account the currency variable) and size-wise (small or big cap companies to stay within the equity, more or less long maturities for government securities, bonds with different level of risk in the corporate sphere).

Making these choices takes time that needs to be subtracted from work or other activities. So, in the end, it is about investing time, before moving the money; but, it is worth it and, frankly speaking, the only option to avoid reckless choices that you may regret afterward.

Chapter 3: Money Excuses

Let's not hide behind the common opinion that you don't have money to invest. Don't get us wrong; you may be in the situation where money is tight and you don't have the resources to make a decisive move in the market. However, you can always control your cash flow and add extra streams of income. These will provide you with more money that you need to save for future investments. We know it is hard, but it is possible, and most millionaires started with nothing.

To us, the mindset is extremely valuable, and in this chapter, we want to debunk once and for all the most recurring excuses people use to avoid or postpone their investments.

1. *"I do not have time to trade."*

One of the most common excuses is to believe that investing can take away most of the precious time we have available. The truth is that we are committing a big error of assessment. Trading does not require a specific amount of time: you can choose how much time you want to dedicate to it. Obviously, the more, the better, but you can even start with a few minutes a day.

Thanks to the advent of the Internet and new technologies, investing is now just a click away, thus reducing not only the costs of negotiation but also the time required.

1. *"I do not have enough money to trade."*

To believe that investing is a subject reserved for those with large quantities of money is one of the worst mistakes we can make. Let's dispel this myth immediately: it is not true that to make money, we need big money. There are affordable financial products that do not require the fortunes of Scrooge McDuck to start planning your future.

From today, it is possible to start trading and investing starting from just 5 euros!

Think about this: €5 equals 5 coffees a week. If we had saved a coffee a day for 5 days a week, since the euros came into force, we would have put aside a "small" sum of €3,865 until the end of the year. If these savings, instead of being forgotten in our piggy bank, were invested in global equity markets, at the end of the year, we would have had €7,493. No savings are therefore insignificant to be invested.

1. *"I do not have the skills to trade."*

One of the reasons that drive us away from investing is to convince ourselves that we do not have the right skills and knowledge. Trading in the forex market may seem apparently tricky, but the truth is that you do not have to be Warren Buffett to start doing it. By investing in mutual funds, for example, our savings are entrusted to a team of expert managers who make the investment choices for us on a daily basis. While we let others manage our money, it is fundamental to learn. Remember that the goal is to become an investor that takes care of his resources.

1. *"I will trade in a few years when I have a higher salary."*

Delaying an investment is not a wise choice, especially considering the benefits of compound interest capitalization. To show you, we have compared two capital accumulation plans: the first invests a sum of €100 a month from the age of 25, while the second invests €200 a month, but starts from 35 years.

In your opinion, which of the two would be able to obtain a higher capital at the age of 70?

The accumulation plan of €100 monthly undertaken for 25 years, will have generated at the age of 70 a capital of €520,000: €50,000 more than the other.

Anticipating the investment not only requires less economic effort, but also allows you to obtain higher earnings compared to a higher investment delayed over time.

1. "Trading is too risky."

None of us wants to lose money, but we do not realize that we are already doing this when we decide not to trade. If the alternative to investing is, in fact, to feel safe by parking our savings on the bank account, inflation could reserve us unpleasant surprises reducing our purchasing power inexorably in the future.

If you trade using portfolio diversification and adopting a long-term time horizon, the chances of losing money are reduced a lot.

Chapter 4: It Is a Question of Money

When it comes to trading strategies, the amount invested cannot be ignored.

This chapter is oriented to the management of assets between €10,000 and €1,000,000. Another premise for reading is to have a clear idea of what is meant by the amount investable.

We will divide our field of action into three bands. All three bands will assume that it has already been done:

- Trade the maximum tax-deductible share in the supplementary pension;
- Stipulate any life insurance—any indicates that all the negative points described in Life Insurance should be considered;
- Deduct from the tradable portion any allowances for false investments (i.e. secondary activities that are genuine alternative works).

The last point is particularly important for investments in real estate and land. As we will see in the operational plans, for assets up to €250,000, a speech on property and land can only be marginal.

The main reasons for the previous statement are:

1. *Such trades often tend not to be real.*

In the modern sense, an investment is such if it requires a minimum allocation of resources (for example, I buy €10,000 of government bonds); otherwise, it is configured as a real activity.

Buying a home that you then rent out is the simplest example.

If we interact directly with the tenant, we are doing a real activity, an alternative to our work, in which we often do not take into account the management costs and the time we spend. Different is the case in which we limit ourselves to buying the house and entrust to a paid external structure the role of administrator of the building. In this second case, what remains is the real gain of the rent. The same applies when buying agricultural land: only by considering it an activity (i.e. cultivating it and managing it with appropriate decisions) will we be able to make the most of it.

1. *These trades minimize management costs only for large capital.*

In fact, the realized capital gains are gross of the taxes and of all the management expenses that serve to maintain the asset in question over the years. For small investments (i.e. a house worth €300,000) inflation, taxes, maintenance costs, etc. reduce the real gain considerably.

Trading Instruments

Instruments investors consider:

1. properties and land;
2. instruments for maximum liquidity (i.e. liquidable in up to 3 months);
3. bonds;
4. stocks; and
5. currencies (forex)

The individual instruments must then be optimized following the instructions given in the following paragraphs.

We must be warned against investing in alternative and typically speculative fields (art, jewelry, etc.) without having a specific capacity. These fields are similar to alternative work: buying a painting, a prestigious watch, or a classic car, hoping for a great revaluation, is completely optimistic if you are not an expert in the sector. On the other hand, if one is, it makes no sense to make it all occasional, but it would make sense to make it at least a second activity.

The proposed management is mainly passive, in the sense that we must follow the trend of our trades not continuously over time, but with periodic checks (e.g. quarterly) to verify whether it is appropriate to disinvest positively. For example, if a currency was bought a year ago at 95.25 and is now worth 99, a 4% gain justifies the sale; if, on the contrary, it has fallen to 94.20, it will put the heart in peace and will be held until its expiration.

From €10,000 to €50,000

I know I am disappointed by those who thought of diversifying, but with such a modest sum, you can only use two tools: forex and bonds. You can use together or, better, use the latter unless the former is no longer advantageous due to a particular economic situation.

From €50,000 to €250,000

Here, the four instruments are all usable, obviously with due consideration.

For buildings and land, it is advisable to include them in the additional quota. If you decide to invest €50,000 in real estate, instead of buying a tiny studio, it makes more sense to buy a bigger house of ownership: the fees on the added quota are less than on a second home, and there wouldn't be all the hassles of managing an asset which, due to its small size, would yield modest yields in any case of a certain management commitment.

Also, in this case, the bonds take the largest share of the investable amount (at least 50%) and can be replaced by the instruments for maximum liquidity only in exceptional cases in which they make more.

The actions deserve separate speech. In theory, with a capital of €250,000, it would be possible to invest in the shareholder, but in practice, it is better to do so by linking the figure to one's age.

If at 30 years, an invested share of 40% can be significant, at the age of 60 it should not exceed 10%. With these data, it is automatic to remember that at the age of 40, a maximum of 30% is invested, and at most 20%, a maximum of 20%.

I propose you the rule of 70: the sum between age and shareholding always makes 70.

Let us remember, however, that investing in the stock is an opportunity, not an obligation.

From €250,000 to €1,000,000

We are now on important figures. Before going into detail, it is necessary to understand "what wind it pulls". Currently, with an economy still in partial crisis, it seems that the situation is this:

Secure bonds and liquidity: ****
Actions: **
Gold: **
Properties: *

This picture will appear disappointing to those who dream of speculating with their capital, but it is certainly the one that protects it most. For those people, forex might not be the best option.

As for property and land, up to 30% of assets can be invested in them, both as an additional share and as an investment in its own right. Many would come to invest up to 100%, but it is a too simplistic solution because, in fact, with such capital, if you want to invest in the brick, it makes more sense to undertake a real second activity. Furthermore, it should be remembered that *a property has value only if you can resell it!*

What in recent years has not been so easy and has produced losses of even 50%, just to fall from the investment made with a little liquidity.

In other words, instead of investing in a couple of luxury apartments in the city center, it is more logical to invest in smaller units by diversifying the risks that are always present on the individual investment. In any case, the crisis in the real estate sector that began in 2008 has, in fact, extinguished optimism that lasted for decades, optimism without a real rational motivation.

Once the portion allocated to property and land has been determined, the amount to be invested in shares must be determined; also, in this case, the maximum is represented by the rule of 70. The remaining part is destined for the bonds.

Chapter 5: An Introduction to Forex and the Difference Between Trading and Investing

Most beginners, investors, and traders have quite confused ideas when approaching the forex market, trading currencies (or options, ETFs, commodities, etc.) or trading in general.

One of the pivotal points that creates confusion in the mind of those interested in making their money work through investments is the lack of understanding of the crucial difference that exists between trading and investing.

The confusion derives from the fact that in the eyes of the investor or the uneducated and non-conscious trader, trading or investing seems to be the same thing.

In reality, although they are united by the desire to make a profit, the two operations arise from different logics and follow different rules.

Those who invest in a measure of the value of what they buy (an action, a house, a business, an object of art, etc.), try to buy it at a discounted or balanced price. Then, the entire operation is based on the prediction or hope that, over time, the good purchased will increase in value and that this increase will automatically be reflected in a corresponding increase in its market price allowing it to be sold for a profit.

An easily understandable example of investment is that of those who buy agricultural land in the expectation that it will then be buildable.

The greatest investors of history, such as the legendary Warren Buffett, are masters in buying "depreciated quality". Of course, their time horizon is never very short, and the value of what they have purchased can remain or even go down for a certain period of time without this causing them to worry excessively.

Who trades, however, does not bet on a change in the value of things. The hard and pure forex trader does not care highly about the objective quality or the nature of what he buys. He is only interested in acquiring it at a price that (in a generally rather short time frame) he plans to grow, even though the value of what he purchased remains perfectly identical.

What makes trading possible is simply the fact that the prices of things (and therefore also investment objects such as shares, bonds, real estate, etc.) may vary regardless of their value due to the law of the application and the offer.

An example out of context of activity comparable to trading is that of the Super Bowl tickets reseller, who obtains the tickets three weeks earlier at regular prices and then resells them at the last moment when he can market them to a much higher price.

On an exchange, it is crucial for an investor to understand what he is buying and what the current and future value of the company he is planning to buy shares is. In other words, investors search quality companies that are currently depreciated.

On the other hand, for a forex trader, it is sufficient to use tools (generally the stock's graph evaluated through technical analysis) that allow him to make a forecast of the future price of the stock regardless of the value of the company and its corporate purpose.

Chapter 6: What You Need to Start Trading in the Forex Market

To start trading, you must meet the following requirements:

- A PC with a stable internet connection
- An online trading platform, to be chosen among those recommended and regulated by us
- All the recommended brokers offer adequate training to all traders whether they are novice traders or experts
- Graphs relating to market quotes in real time
- Economic news
- Comments and operational suggestions
- A great desire to learn

Today, thanks to online trading it will be possible to obtain profits that can reach up to 70% based on the chosen broker and a fair trading preparation, without which one risks losing the entire capital invested. Therefore we advise you scrupulously to apply and follow all the advice that your broker provides you.

In addition, thanks to the several materials that can be found in this book you can start learning what the right terms of online trading are, how you can invest in the forex market, etc.

When investing in the forex market, you can do mainly two different types of transactions:

- Long operations (upward investment)
- Short transactions (downward investment)

In other words, when you are trading, you can buy currencies and sell currencies. The goal, however, remains the same: to make a profit. When you want to buy, you will only get a profit if the value of the currency will be increased when we want to sell it. For example, we buy 100 lots of currency when it is worth $1.1 each, and then we sell them when they're worth $1.2 each. The price difference multiplied by the number of lots equals our profit.

When you want to sell, it becomes a bit more complicated. In short transactions, it is the broker that lends us the number of shares on which we want to invest on the downside. For example, the broker can lend us €1,000 listed at $1.23 each. The securities that the broker lends us for a short transaction are sold immediately while the profit remains "frozen" in their trading account.

This profit will be used to buy back the same amount of currency that the broker had lent us because we have to return this currency to the broker. In that case, we will have a gain if the value of the currency has fallen.

The difference between the initial sale of the securities lent and the expense to repurchase them is +€500: in this case, that is our profit. If, on the other hand, the value of the currency increases, we will have to spend more money than those earned from the initial sale of the pre-arranged securities: in this case, we will suffer a loss.

Chapter 7: Not Only Forex

The main method for investing in the forex market, therefore, remains the classic forex market. When you operate on the forex market, you are actually buying and selling currencies.

However, over the years, other financial instruments have been introduced to invest in forex and currencies indices on the forex exchange. We are talking about CFD (contract for difference) and binary options. The main feature of these two financial instruments is the following: when you use them to invest in forex, you will not actually own the lots you are investing in.

That said, for those who do not intend to do trading online, it could make little sense. Let's try to clarify. Both CFDs and binary options are contracts between investors and brokers. It's not like the classic forex market, where traders buy and sell among themselves. In CFDs and binary options, the asset movement (in this case, the buying and selling of currencies) does not take place.

CFDs and binary options are used to speculate on the performance of the value of equity securities. If the trader's forecast is correct, the operation will lead to a profit; vice versa, if the trader's prediction is wrong, the operation will lead to a loss. So, the mode of operation is similar to the stock market: if I invest on the upside, whether I do it with CFDs or actually buy currencies, I only earn money if the value increases.

As we explained in the previous paragraphs, CFDs are also derivative instruments, so they are used to speculate on the performance of asset values. This means that when you buy and sell CFDs, you will never own the asset traded (as opposed to classic forex trading).

Moreover, with CFDs, as with binary options, it is possible to trade on:

1. Equity securities

2. Equity indices
3. Forex currencies pairs
4. Commodities
5. ETF

Leverage plays an essential role in CFD trading: through leverage, we can literally multiply the value of our investment. Just to give an example, if you use a lever of 1:100 and invest €100, you can move well €10,000 (using only your hundred!). All these are made possible thanks to the leverage, which is a sort of "loan" (if we can define it) by the broker, which you can invest more money than you really have.

This means that your earnings, but also your losses, will be calculated not on the €100 you really invested, but on the €10,000, you will have invested. Therefore, the lever not only can amplify the gains but also the losses. To see an example of CFD trading, we will refer you to our article on how to trade CFDs in equities with eToro. eToro is one of the leading CFD brokers, very suitable also for non-professional traders and those who want to approach the world of online trading (thanks to the free and unlimited demo account offer).

But if we talk about eToro, we cannot talk about Social Trading. For those who do not know, eToro was the first broker to have introduced Social Trading in CFDs. With Social Trading, it is possible to invest by copying (automatically) the operations carried out by the other traders registered on the eToro platform. All you need is a couple of clicks to find the traders to follow, choose the amount to invest, and you're done. In this way, even novice traders can exploit the knowledge and experience of professional traders, copying their operations.

The online trading strategies are based on the study of mathematical and graphic analysis that can suggest the trader the best moment to buy and sell. As we have seen today, it is possible to invest in the stock market, choosing between trading binary options and trading with the forex market.

Precise right away that there is no suitable trading strategy for all traders, but there are different trading strategies based on traders and their style of trading. Therefore, it is possible to customize different online trading strategies by their trading objectives, their intellectual and psychological abilities.

We also recommend using two proven techniques not to turn winnings into losses:

1. **Stop loss**: establishes a maximum loss that you are willing to suffer
2. **Take profit**: you place a dynamic exit level that rises slowly

Similar to Forex Trading: Penny Stocks

Investing is something that many people are interested in. They want to see how much their money can grow for them and some even want to see if they can make this a full-time income rather than working their regular jobs. There is a variety of investments that you can make. Some people keep it safe and place their money in a savings account, while others go with a retirement plan. Some will go with real estate and choose one of those options when the market is good, and others like to start their own business, get into the stock market, or invest in a friend who is doing something new. The options can be endless when it comes to starting a new investment, and picking out the right one for you can be the hardest part of getting started.

One investment type that you may want to try is the penny stock. This is a type of stock that starts out really low, at no more than $1 for each of the shares. According to the Securities and Exchange Commission in the United States, a penny stock is one that will trade at no more than $5 a share, but most of them will be less than that.

A penny stock can bring about a huge profit to those who know how to use it, but not a popular option as it works off the regular stock market and is often used when a company is really desperate for some money. There is the potential for large losses, even if you purchase at a small rate, but if you can read the market, there is the potential to see a great deal and make a good profit in the process.

One of the best ways to ensure that you aren't taking a big loss on these stocks is to be careful who you purchase from. Some unscrupulous people will make a big purchase of penny stocks to help raise the price. They will use fake press releases, websites, stock message boards, and more to talk up the penny stock so more people will make a purchase and then the price goes up even more. Then, they sell the stocks at the inflated price, making themselves a lot of money while everyone else will not be able to find any buyers and will either have to hold onto the stock or sell it at a loss.

The good news is that the penny stock does need to meet some standards to prevent the process above, which is known as pump and dump (P&D). Inside the United States, these stocks need to have a price, market capitalization, and minimum shareholder equity. Remember that even if the stock you are looking at is below $5, it will not be a penny stock unless it is traded off of the stock exchange.

The Good About Penny Stocks

We spent a little time talking about some of the things that you will need to avoid when using penny stocks and looking to invest in these opportunities. If you are careful about watching the market and seeing what is going on before you make a purchase, you should be able to figure out when a pump and dump scheme is going on. If something looks like it is rising in price too quickly, or you see that there was only one buyer of a large amount of penny stocks with just one company, or you feel like this person is really trying to pressure someone into making a purchase that doesn't look like the best, it is a good idea to go with a different option for the penny stocks.

The good news is that you can do well in penny stocks, you just have to keep your head and make sure that you aren't trying to rush into something that doesn't make sense or that has a lot of red flags all over it. One of the best ways to get the most out of your penny stocks is to learn how to do your research before making any purchases.

There are many things that you will be able to research about a penny stock before you get started. For example, start by looking at the corporate website for the company you want to work with. This provides you with a good idea about the company because a lot of information can be there. You should then look at the balance sheet of the company to see how many debts the company is dealing with; if there are too many debts, the company may be trying to sell the penny stocks to get out of debt, but if they haven't learned how to control that debt, throwing more money over to them won't help. You want to pick penny stocks out from companies that are profitable or the ones who can reduce their losses properly and will not take on large amounts of debt to keep running.

Penny stocks can be a great form of investing if you are looking to get started with an option or you want to expand out your portfolio out to make your money work a little harder. We are going to take a look at more parts about penny stocks and how you will be able to make them go to work for you.

So before we get into some of the basics of trading in penny stocks, we need to take some time to understand the different methods that companies can list themselves in this kind of market. Remember that, while there are rules for penny stocks, they are not considered part of the stock market, so working with them is going to be a bit different than what you are used to. Here we are going to talk about how a company can list in Pink Sheets and what this means for you as the investor.

Listing in Pink Sheets

For a company to get started with penny stocks, they will first need to file the Form 211 to be listed in Pink Sheets. This is a privately held corporation, compared to the other option (which we will talk about later) over-the-counter Bulletin Board, which is a service that is owned by the NASDAQ. Many companies use Pink Sheets to work with, and when they fill out the Form 211, they will need to submit it over to the OTC Compliance Unit. The market maker is going to process the listing for the company. The broker and dealer will be able to quote a price for this company, as long as the company is pretty transparent. However, some companies won't commit to this transparency because they won't submit their current information on business financials.

For companies that are listed using the Pink Sheets, you will find that they are small and thin traders. These companies will not have to work with the SEC during the trading time, and they don't have to file their periodic reports. Now, some of them will do this filing to show what they are doing and to help the investor feel more comfortable with working with them, but this is not a requirement. In many cases, it can be difficult to get information to understand companies that are on the Pink Sheets because you just don't have the information that is needed to get started.

The Benefits of Trading Pink Sheets

Even though the companies who use Pink Sheets are not required to be transparent or file periodic updates, an investor is usually going to find some pretty good options to trade in penny stocks with these Pink Sheets. You have the possibility of getting a high return because these are the volatile stocks. There are also some companies in this group that used to be strong, but for some reason or another, had to leave the major exchanges because of a strict requirement they no longer met. They may still be good companies to trade with, and you could make some good profits from it.

It is also possible to find obscure companies to trade with to help that company grow before they move over to one of the major exchanges. You would be able to invest with these companies early on, and this could give you a huge reward later as they start to grow and move over to the stock exchange.

In addition, the Pink Sheets system has a tier system that helps you to differentiate between the companies that are there. This helps you to figure out which stocks are higher risk and which ones are lower risk based on the classifications that are set. You can pick whichever risk setting that you are happy and comfortable with, but as a beginner, it is nice to know which ones fall into each category to help you make a decision.

If you want to use the Pink Sheets as part of your trading, you need to make sure that you really do your research. Pink Sheets is not going to provide you with much information about the companies you are trading with, and if you just randomly pick a company, you are increasing your risk and making it likely that you will lose all of your money.

The Classifications System

As mentioned before, the Pink Sheets system has a classification for each of the companies that trade using it. This makes it easier to determine whether a company is a high risk or low risk and you can make your decisions based on this. Some of the tiers that are found inside of the classification system include:

- *Trusted Tier*

Inside of the trusted tier in Pink Sheets, you will find the international as well as American companies that are considered trustworthy and investor friendly. The companies from other countries are going to be on the international exchange, but they can still fit into this trusted tier. The companies in this tier have not met the requirements to be on the regular stock exchange, but this is usually because of one or two small things since the stock exchange is so strict.

However, even though these companies were not able to get onto the stock exchange, they were able to pass an independent audit. This list sometimes includes companies in American that pass the standards needed for NASDAQ but they aren't submitting SEC reports, and so they would be moved over to Pink Sheets instead.

- *Transparent Tier*

This is a tier that will send in SEC reports and, sometimes, will also include those that are in Over-the-Counter Bulletin Boards. These are highly trusted companies because you will be able to see some of their financial reports as well as other information that is required for them to be good with the SEC. You will be able to do your research on these companies because it is provided to you and can save a lot of guesswork and hassle when choosing the penny stocks you want to work with.

- *Distressed Tier*

Companies in this tier of Pink Sheets are ones that provide limited information for the investor to look at and, often, they are not following the guidelines that are set out by Pink Sheets. These companies may not even send out updated information to the SEC as they should, but some of them will work with the OTC disclosures. Not all of these are bad to work with, but sometimes you need to be wary because they aren't sending out the right information and some of them have been bankrupt.

- *Dark Tier*

This is the tier that you will really need to watch out for because it could cause some issues. Companies inside of this particular tier aren't sending in any information about their business. They aren't filing information with either the SEC or the OTC Disclosure service, and they haven't done so over at least the last six months, making it really hard for the investor to have any idea how this stock is doing. Some companies get into this tier that are also failing with transparency in the market, or they don't have a market marker.

- *Toxic Tier*

As a new investor or any investor for that matter, it is best to stay out of the toxic tier. Companies that are in this tier will often rely on marketing strategies that are fraudulent such as using promotions that are questionable or sending out a lot of spam to name a few. These can also include some companies that are subjected to large corporate events that disrupt them or they may have a suspension by the government. In some cases, these will not actually have their own business operations and can be really dangerous to send your money to.

Taking a look at these different types of tiers inside this system can help you to make a more informed choice when it comes to working in the Pink Sheets. You will be able to see these rankings with any of the companies that you choose to go with, and if you pick the one with the highest reputation, it becomes easier to get good returns on investments.

How to Make Decisions in Pink Sheets

So, now that we know a bit more about Pink Sheets and how they work, it is time to learn how to do the trading decisions. When picking out a penny stock inside of Pink Sheets, you are going to be limited on information and technical analysis of most of the companies. There are also some issues on occasion because there isn't a central exchange that you can use to buy and trade these stocks. This is why it is best to start out with a broker and dealer who will be able to walk you through this process.

As the investor, you will need to do a fundamental analysis of any company that you want to invest in, even if they are not sending the information your way. You can look at the different companies and their past history, and you can look to see if there are some hidden gems that other people will miss out on right now, but which will make the stock better later on. With some good research, you will quickly be able to narrow down the choices that you want to use.

Working with Pink Sheets can be one way to get started on penny stocks, but you need to be careful. Some of the companies are great and will provide you with information to pick them; many of these are working to get to the stock exchange, but for some small reason or another, they are not quite there yet, and these are pretty safe options to go with. But there are also companies on the Pink Sheets that won't provide any information, and some that are even fraudulent, so you need to be careful about the companies that you invest in to help keep your portfolio strong and growing.

Investing with OTC Bulletin Boards

Another option that you can choose to invest for your penny stocks is the Over-the-Counter Bulletin Boards or the OTC Boards. This one, at least inside of the United States, is operated through the Financial Industry Regulatory Authority and it will hold many of the stocks and securities that are not found on the NASDAQ or other stock exchanges. You will need to work with brokers and dealers to order the penny stocks since this is not an electronic method, and it can be pretty secure to work with.

This type of penny stock is usually seen as a little more secure because they are required to send in financial information and to be transparent. It is regulated a bit more, and often the companies that are on this one will be here because they didn't meet some small requirement to be on the exchange. All of the companies that are listed on these bulletin boards will need to report their information to the SEC, but they don't have to include as much information as they would on the stock exchange, and they can leave our information on their market capitalization, minimum share price, governance, and more.

These are usually seen as a bit more secure because these companies have to send in information and report to the SEC while the companies on the Pink Sheets could do this reporting, but they didn't have to. Many beginners in penny stocks will choose to go with this option because it allows them to learn a bit more about the company that they want to invest in, making it easier to pick a smart investment on their end of things.

Both the OTC Bulletin Boards and the Pink Sheets can be great places to start to find the penny stock that you want to work with.

Some of the options can be a bit risky, but as a good investor, it is up to you to step in and do the research to find this information out. You are going to find risky investments no matter where you are, whether on or off the stock market or in other forms of investing, but you need to find the one that works the best for you and has the right risk to reward ratio that you are comfortable with. Both of these trading methods have their own systems to help you to make these decisions, and if you are working with a broker and a dealer, you should have the support that you need to make the right decisions.

Here are some suggestions that you should follow when you are trading forex and other financial instruments.

Because of the continuous ups and downs that have involved international stock exchanges in recent months, many have begun to ask themselves the fateful question: "Is investing in shares still the best strategy to multiply my savings?".

The financial markets, in general, can be an extraordinary opportunity: not only stocks but also cryptocurrencies or forex can give great satisfaction even if, however, it is necessary to have preparation before going into rash choices.

The 17 Golden Lessons Before Entering the Stock Market

In this chapter, we will go deep into the subject and discover the golden lessons that every investor should know before entering the stock market.

1. **Easy money is like Santa Claus: it does not exist.**

Who promises to quintuple your assets without sweating is not more than a seller of smoke. Investing in the stock market is not a joke. To achieve the investment goals, you have set yourself to avoid risky securities, focusing on something more stable, lasting, and profitable. In the recipe for success, in addition to a serious knowledge of the stock markets, there is also the sentimental component (for those investing, there is no room for panic but a lot of patience) and even a bit of luck.

1. **Gold and cash do not give interest.**

Everyone knows that cash does not disappear, but after the bizarre maneuvers of the European Central Bank (which brought negative returns on the single currency), we can be even more certain that investing in cash does not create any interest. The dream of all is to be able to accumulate that amount of money enough to enjoy a quiet retirement, but the closer it gets to the time x, the more the small investor tends to panic. Hence, the reckless choices to invest in cash or in commodities such as gold which, although it proves to be more stable than fiat, cannot hold the same value forever.

Just think that in the last luster, the value of the most precious metal fell by 34.8%.

1. A winning strategy has ingredients.

One of the main factors of success on the stock exchange is sentiment. Patience, foresight, and prudence are the three basic ingredients of winning strategies, but it is also true that a little risk never hurts.

If the money we have invested on a certain stock does not return, you should look around and find some slightly riskier but at least profitable activity, with the hope that an important injection of money into the markets can restart the economy by stimulating productivity and development.

1. Establish investment goals.

Before starting to invest then embark on a challenging and long path, you must have a clear mind of where you want to go. It depends on personal aspirations, on the trust that one has for himself, and on many other factors. However, the main choice is between protecting capital and making it grow. Under certain conditions, the stock exchange also lends itself to the speculative approach. Who wants to start could also establish concrete objectives such as buying a good or a service. In any case, the rule is always the same: to understand where you want to arrive.

1. Establish the degree of risk tolerance.

This is probably the most important phase. The stock market is extremely varied and allows numerous approaches, from the prudent and static to the dynamic and courageous.

This is why it is always good to establish one's degree of tolerance. Based on this decision, further choices will be made until the real investment is realized. Investor profiles depend on personal characteristics and their economic situation. If you are a simple worker, do not sail in gold and maybe those who invest are the savings of a lifetime, it is good to give up any speculative ambitions. The degree of tolerance determines the risk that you intend to run and the strategy that will be adopted later.

1. Study.

The information issue should not be forgotten. The stock market is complex and structurally risky, so we need to be cautious. The risk is to lose capital in a short period of time. Therefore, it is necessary to undertake a training course that confers at least the theoretical tools. The topic of the study should consist of both the investment modalities—how it is invested in the concrete—and the economic environment in general.

As for the sources, including paper texts, successful books, and the Internet, you are spoiled with choices.

The study activity, however, never abandons the investor even when he has become an expert. Pressing is the need to update continuously, but also to inquire about everything that gravitates around the securities in the portfolio.

1. Choose the long term.

Investing in the stock market should not be an act of just a few months or even a few years. It must be a continuous activity. It is only through patience and perseverance that it is possible to make substantial profits. This means that you need to build a long-term version, which looks at least for the next five years (even if ten years is more suitable). This means that it is okay not to give in to the temptation to sell the securities as soon as the prices start to fall. Life is worth the saying, "Laugh well who laughs last".

1. Monitor.

If you opt for a long-term vision, as you should, then it is essential to monitor the status of your investment. Not everyone knows that control and monitoring begin before the investment itself. In particular, it is necessary to establish a benchmark (i.e. a yardstick) using where it is possible to really understand whether we are on the right path or not. Finally, it is good to make a periodic comparison between the expected results and the real ones. In the beginning, there is a strong temptation to abandon oneself to discouragement, also because the results tend to arrive farther with time.

A general consideration can be made on the segment within which to operate. Everything depends on risk tolerance. If this is very low, you should address those segments that, by their nature, do not suffer from the crisis. The reference is to those goods whose consumption is practically mandatory, such as food and pharmaceuticals. Investing in pharmaceutical companies' actions will not make you rich, but is a very useful asset to protect capital. Strangely enough, but up to a certain point, the high-tech segment (e.g. mobile phones, social networks, etc.) also plays a similar role. Investing in the stock market can be a business that can increase its capital. In addition to technical knowledge, we need some moral skills: patience, perseverance, lucidity, foresight. All qualities that must be cultivated and that can make the difference. Vice versa, it will never give good fruits if an approach is based on imprudence and haste from the frenzy of profit.

1. Use the leverage.

What unfortunately many traders do not consider is investing in the stock market or trading online using leverage. To invest in the stock market with little money, it is necessary to deepen the study of this tool, which will allow us to expose our capital to a huge risk. We recommend the use of leverage only on a reduced capital, carried out concurrently also with a rationalized use of stop loss and take profit. Also, you must always have your budget under control using careful Money Management. Finally, before investing in the stock market, you need to study the markets and all the financial instruments on which you want to invest in.

1. You do not need to be a finance guru to invest in the stock market.

Apparently, we are not telling you that the market should not be studied or that there must be a basis for training. Who applies himself and follows the markets, deepening the subject, will always know more than others.

So we always recommend following the training path of your broker, which will allow you not to take missteps throughout the investment process. Taking advantage of the online trading demo platforms, it is possible to simulate the investment and understand where mistakes are made and avoid them when investing with a real account.

1. **Use only trusted brokers.**

We believe that the stock market is not a market for everyone but a few! Above all, we cannot recommend the investments on the stock exchange to those subjects are not inclined to study at least basic and training. In this case, it is better to let go of one's own, as it is not possible to rely only on luck.

Our advice is to stay away if you do not have and do not want to learn specific skills. If you do not have a basic education, all the savings you invest will lose them in less than a month. On the contrary, instead, we recommend investing in the stock market with online trading and regulated brokers. This is because, being regulated and being subjected to strict controls, they do not put capital at risk and also the broker will provide you with a fair and complete formation. In the link below, you will find a complete list of regulated and authorized brokers to invest with:

https://www.allfxbrokers.com/brokers/usa-clients.

1. **Learn technical analysis.**

Technical analysis is the study of price trends with the use of graphs. The interest of a technical analyst is to look for the graphic configurations that are drawn by price movements.

The market trend is evaluated to understand possible future price movements.

The pure technical analysis is not based on any fundamental of the underlying activity but applies a series of technical tools drawn on the chart to allow for future courses.

On the chart, price movements are usually represented by bars or candles, allowing price analysis in a certain period called 'timeframe'.

On a candle, the body or the central part represents the difference between opening and closing in a given period. The shadow (i.e., the top and bottom segment) represent the difference between the maximum and the minimum of the period considered and the opening or closing of the candle. We can have monthly, daily, 1 hour, 5 minutes, or even shorter candles. The different colors of the candles indicate a rise or fall in the period. Usually, a green candle represents a rise in prices, which means that the closing price of the candle is higher than the opening one, while the red candle represents a drop.

The levels of the chart where prices find an obstacle are called 'levels of support or resistance'. A 'support' is the level at which a bearish price halts its downfall and potentially 'rebounds' up again. The most significant support is repeatedly tested and becomes the level of support from a technical point of view. The 'resistance' is the opposite of the support. It is the level at which a rising price finds an obstacle to rise further and shows a decline instead. Even a resistance tested several times takes on higher strategic importance.

When prices determine an important level of support but then violate it downwards, this level of support becomes an important area of resistance. The same goes for a resistance that if violated on the upside turns into a significant level of support.

There are so many indicators used by technical analysts to try and predict the next price movements. One of the most used indicators is the 'simple moving average', which is calculated on a certain amount of price data and is mobile because it moves from period to period.

Given an average of a certain time frame, the most recent data is added each time, eliminating the last data in the series from the calculation. The moving average can be used as a support or dynamic resistance. The most used periods on the daily chart for the moving average are 50, 100, and 200. If prices show a significant uptrend, the moving average will be an important short-term or medium-term support, inversely if prices show a bearish trend the average mobile will be a significant dynamic resistance.

1. Learn fundamental analysis.

Unlike the previous one, it is based on the study of the company and its reference market. In practice, it is based on balance sheet data, on management's ability and credibility, on trends in the specific sector in which the company operates. In this case, one must also consider the following: *value investing*, *growth investing*, and *investment*.

All traders have a different investing style. Every trader has his own investment techniques, and each has his own particular techniques, as well as particular tricks and particular "secrets".

But do not be fooled by the strange idea of being able to learn how to invest by reading articles on the internet: this is impossible. You can find excellent advice but not the magic formula. At most, you could clear your mind and give yourself a general orientation, but to get serious you need longer and more in-depth things.

1. Analyze the state of the market.

Closely connected to the concept of technical analysis and fundamental analysis is the concept of analysis of the general market. It does not matter whether you are a professional investor or a beginner, this will be the most difficult step you need to understand.

In practice, it is pure art applied to scientific instruments. You must first understand and analyze the market for the sole purpose of formulating a plausible development scenario. This also means accumulating an enormous amount of data and statistics regarding the performance of the securities and developing the "sensitivity" necessary to choose the truly relevant ones. If you put this into practice, you will also understand why many investors buy the shares of a particular company and not of another one.

At the same time, we always advise you to observe the products you have at home. Although this element may seem unusual, it is very important to understand that you have direct knowledge of many products and not others. In practice, it will allow you to perform a quick and intuitive analysis of the financial performance of the manufacturing companies, comparing them with those of their competitors.

Before investing, you must reflect on the products examined. For example, try to imagine the economic conditions for which you might decide to stop buying them or increase or decrease your stocks. This is a great exercise to get a feeling of what an average person needs and treats as "important".

1. **Create an investment plan.**

This is a very important step: you have to create an investment plan. But to do that, you must first of all fully understand why you want to invest.

You must know how much you can invest in and how much you want to invest in achieving your goals. You must also have clear ideas about what your goals are. To do this, you could always use an Excel sheet or even a special tool to calculate how much you will have to spend to achieve your goals.

Based on the income you can afford to invest then, calculate the type of investment. You cannot claim to get $10,000 from an investment if what you can afford to invest in trading online or on the stock exchange or even in other systems does not exceed €1,000 euros. Everything must be proportionate. Start small and build it up over time.

1. **Understand asset location.**

Defined as the distribution of liquidity in the various investment, instruments available should vary depending on the stage of life in which you are into.

This means that, if you are young, the percentage of your investment portfolio relative to the shares will have to be higher. On the contrary, if you have a solid and well-paid career, your job is like an obligation! You can use it to guarantee long-term income. This allows you to allocate most of your financial portfolio in shares. At the same time, you have to understand that if you have a job whose remuneration is not predictable, as in the case where you are self-employed, then you have to allocate most of your financial portfolio in more stable products; in this case, it is better to invest in bonds, perhaps government bonds and not in shares.

At the same time, however, you must consider that the actions allow faster growth of your invested assets but as such entails a greater risk.

1. Study the financial risk.

Another element to take into consideration when choosing to invest in a stock exchange is the financial risk. We could define it as the risk linked to the fact that investment can go wrong. This also assumes that the yield is lower than expected or may even go red. So, be careful not to underestimate this element.

On the other hand, it is an element that is not easy to understand and accept. At the same time, it is not infrequent and it is due to different dimensions that it is always good to know.

The financial risk has different facets. In practice, it could be of a different nature:

- Specific: linked to the performance of the single instrument we purchased.
- Systematic: linked to the oscillation of the financial market of the manager; linked to the skills of those who manage yours.
- Money-related: be it an investment fund manager, or a financial planner or consultant to whom you have been entrusted.
- Market timing: the possibility of making mistakes when entering and/or leaving the market.
- Liquidity: the possibility of having to sell a stock that has little market (it is called a little liquid title) and to have a low price.
- Currency: when buying a security denominated in foreign currency, the yield will also depend on the ratio between the currency and the euro.

Analyzed according to these elements, financial risk is a bit more complex than the simple possibility that things go wrong. Understanding it and knowing how to manage these different risks can, therefore, shift the odds that things are going well in our favor.

Chapter 8: How Much Money to Start With?

Many people ask themselves this question: how much money do they need to invest in the forex market? An entirely legitimate question, but whose answer varies according to many factors. First of all, consider how you have decided to invest in currencies. The classic forex market requires capital of a certain size, usually including (at least) between €5,000-€10,000 to start investing in the forex market.

If you do not have these figures or do not feel ready to invest them, you can use other financial instruments such as CFDs and binary options. In both cases, the minimum capital to invest is really limited: we usually speak of €100-200 to open an online trading account and have access to a trading platform to invest. Apparently, no one forbids you to start investing a larger amount: our advice, especially if you have never done online trading before, is to invest a maximum of €1,000 in your first CFD trading account or binary options.

Regardless of how you have decided to invest in the forex market, however, remember to choose only figures that you can afford to lose. What does it mean? It means that you have to invest in figures that will not put your financial stability at risk. In other words, do not invest "too big" figures for your pockets.

Another topic that must always be dealt with when it comes to investing in the forex market is the risk. Let's clarify it: trading online, as investing in the forex market, is risky. Risk is a factor that cannot be eliminated. Anyone who tells you that online trading and investing in the stock market is risk-free and easy is lying shamelessly. Trading online is risky, as it can result in the loss of your capital (in case of bad decisions).

Management-Money-And-Risk

All investment activities are risky; whether it's the real estate market, opening a business, or starting a start-up or online trading, the risk is always present. The important thing is to know how to manage the risk factor so that it can be reduced and controlled. Nevertheless, remember that you will never be able to eliminate the risk factor completely. It will always be present in all your future forex exchange transactions.

This means that sooner or later, you will lose money by investing in the forex market. After all, no one is perfect: being able to make only profitable investments is impossible. We must accept the fact that suffering losses "is part of the game". But the important thing is to earn more than what you can lose. If, for example, out of 10 investment transactions you miss 2, but you earn from the remaining 8, you can say that you have reached an excellent goal (and profit).

Fix yourself with the idea of not wanting to lose money by investing in the stock market; it will not help if you're going to start trading online. Professional investors know very well that losses must be learned to accept, and aim to limit their number (check the term well: limit, do not eliminate). In this way, by limiting losses, profits will increase—the goal that every trader should operate on the forex exchange.

What is the minimum capital requested to invest in the stock market? In this chapter, we will try to answer this question, with attention to the type of operation and market. First of all, we specify that when we talk about the minimum capital to invest in the stock market, we are talking about something very different from the minimum capital to invest in forex. While the investment in forex has an essentially speculative activity, in the stock exchange investment, dividends, coupons, and long-term investments are also to be assessed. Now, let's analyze how much it takes to invest in the stock market.

As mentioned, the minimum capital to invest in the stock market depends mainly on the type of operation that you intend to have. We can say with absolute certainty that the smaller the duration of the investment is, the lesser the required capital is. We explain this statement in detail:

If we operate with a maximum daily duration, it is presumable that every evening we close all open positions, so our minimum capital to invest in the stock market, even without leverage, may even be only €1,000, allowing at least one transaction per day. Operating with leveraging the minimum capital to invest in the stock exchange may be lower, even a few euros if we use high leverage. It seems evident that if the duration of our investment will be semi-annual, the minimum capital to invest in the stock market will have to be decidedly higher so as not to be in the sad condition of being able to operate once every six months.

So far, we have talked of minimum capital to invest in the stock market exclusively from the number of possible transactions, but it is not so simple. The minimum capital to invest in the stock market should be sufficient to diversify our exposure to avoid large losses. The ideal situation would be to invest in at least three markets with only two market transactions. It goes without saying that with a very short duration leverage operation, the minimum capital to invest in the stock market will be from a few thousand euro, while for half-year transactions the capital will necessarily have to be higher. So far, we have talked about optimal operations. The minimum capital to invest in the stock market will depend very much on your risk profile. The greater your risk appetite, the higher your leverage will be, and therefore you will be able to invest with a smaller capital.

Chapter 9: Compound Interest and Forex

Earning more means being paid more. We usually think that others should pay us more if we want to make more money, but this is not always true. We can earn more even if we pay ourselves more, and not the others.

This is a fundamental principle underlying the financial success, first disclosed in 1926 by George Samuel Clason through his book entitled *The Richest Man in Babylon*, a great motivational classic.

The principle states that part of what you earn must be maintained. Putting aside at least 10% of what you earn—and making that money inaccessible to ordinary expenses and possibly even extraordinary expenses—you can increase this amount exponentially over time. Considering any investments, thanks to the power of the compound investment, the amount saved or invested over the years can become important. In fact, many people can earn more and build their assets by paying themselves first. It is a true and effective principle today as it was in 1926.

Yet, as this 10% formula is easy, people are unwilling to listen to it and apply it. This is because you are usually looking for tricks to get rich quickly, and you do not have a medium to long-term vision. On the other hand, having a long-term investment plan is a solid foundation on which to build one's own economic stability. And you can start earning more by paying yourself first from today. The earlier you start, the quicker you will build your financial success.

Using the Power of Compound Interest

To earn more, you can take advantage of the compound interest. Here's how it works: if you invest €1,000 at a 5% interest, you will earn €50 of interest, and at the end of the first year, you will have a total investment of €1,050. If you leave both the initial investment and the interest earned on the current account, you will receive a 5% interest the following year over €1,050, or €52.50. In the third year, you will earn 5% out of 1,102.50, and so on. At this rate, within 15-30 years your money will turn into an amount well above the sum invested initially. But precisely how much does the invested capital grow? The Italian mathematician Luca Pacioli explained it in the 15th century: any capital doubles in a number of years equal to 72 divided by the interest rate. Returning to our example: if the interest is at 5% per year, we divide 72 by 5; which makes 14.4 (i.e., in 14 years and 4 months the initial capital doubles). The sooner you start, the bigger the result will be, as you will have more time for the interest you capitalize on produce its powerful magic. Start now to save and invest for your future, even if you do not have a large sum. You do not need to have an extra sum of money. You can start with any amount and grow it over time.

The Secret of Paying of Yourself First

If you want to earn more money by paying yourself first, you have to make savings and investment a central part of your financial management, just like the mortgage payment. Get accustomed to saving a fixed percentage (at least 10%) of your monthly income and investing it in special savings account that you decide not to touch. Ideally, this step would be automatic, such as a fixed monthly deduction on your paycheck. The automation will ensure that you will not have to rely on your self-discipline and your ability to save will not be affected by your mood from domestic emergencies or otherwise. Continue to increase that account until you have saved enough to invest the sum accumulated in bonds, in a mutual fund or real estate (spending money on rent without building any assets is really a waste). Let your investments build your assets over time, and try to live with what remains after you have paid yourself. If you want to spend, try to earn more to afford it. But never put your hands on your savings to finance a more ambitious lifestyle. The ideal would be for your investments to grow to the point where you could live with interest, if necessary. Only then will you really be financially autonomous and free.

If you want to earn more, you need to create assets, not liabilities. Rather than spending all the money you earn by enriching someone else, invest in assets that produce other income (stocks, bonds, real estate, gold, etc.). Then when your money starts to grow, educate yourself further about the best way to invest your money. Stay informed about news about investment opportunities and remember to protect what is yours through a good insurance policy. Do not blindly trust who will manage your money, but always try to improve your financial education. This will make you a financially prepared person ready to get rich. Once you understand this, money will follow.

What is compound interest? Not everyone may know how to respond immediately to this question. If everyone knows what the simple interest is (i.e., the one that withdraws at the end of the agreed time unit), fewer are those who know what the compound interest is, how it works, and, most importantly, how to take advantage of it.

The example of a bank account is enlightening.

If on 1 January, I have a net rate of 1% on my account, at the end of the year I have €101. A euro more is added to the capital and, if the conditions do not change, at the end of the second year, I will not have €102, but €102 and a cent where the cent represents 1% of the euro accumulated after the first year.

So far, everything is clear, but most of us cannot calculate the compound interest of investment and tend to treat it as simple interest. This is due to its slow start, that, especially with small capital, tend to be treated as "irrelevant". However, there is nothing more wrong that an investor could do.

If, for example, after 5 years of investment, my capital of €100 is now €140, we are led to believe that the interest was 8% per year.

This is incorrect because, in doing so, we do not take into account that at the end of each period the interest accumulate has gone to increase capital. If the interest had really been 8%, composing the 5 years we would have had

Initial capital: €100

- 1st year: €108
- 2nd year: €116.64
- 3rd year: €125.97
- 4th year: €136.04
- 5th year: €146.93

The difference (€6.93) represents almost 7% of the total. As you can see, it is easy to take dazzle (and worse, even "suffer", if for some reason we are offered a simple interest for a compound interest).

The Maths Behind Compound Interest: An Easy Example

Suppose we have an initial capital of €1,000. The capital yields a Y% interest and this interest is calculated on an annual basis.

What will be the value of the investment after X years?

The calculation formula is as follows:

(1) $IV = CP (1 + Y) \wedge X$

IV is the value of the investment after X years, while CP is the initial capital. Y is expressed as a percentage, i.e. 0.04 indicates 4%. The symbol $\wedge$ is the symbol of elevation to power.

The inverse calculation tends to find the Y interest of an investment that now (net of inflation) is worth IV against a CP capital invested X periods (years) ago. The formula is:

(2) $Y = (IV / CP) \wedge (1 / X) - 1$

Suppose that, after inflation, €1,000 invested 5 years ago are now worth €1,400, you immediately have that the yield was 6.96%.

Let's take a look at another example:

Marie has just taken the salary and can finally buy the air conditioner she needs.

But her friend Julie calls her to tell her that she has an urgent need that she cannot cope with immediately and asks her to borrow €1,000.

Marie is undecided because this would mean waiting another month before she can make her purchase.

To resolve the issue, the two girls agree on the loan provided that Julie returns the money to Mary with a 5% interest (the numbers are purely random for the example).

In this way, Marie has a greater incentive to have to delay her purchase.

When Julie returns the sum loaned, she will receive €1,050 instead of €1,000.

The following month, Marie can then buy the air conditioner and, to celebrate, use the accumulated interest (€50) to go out to dinner with her boyfriend.

In short, in the end, this recognition for the delayed use was not bad!

Now that we understand the concept behind the rate of interest, it is good to enter a little more in detail and make some distinctions.

In this regard, we can divide the interest rate into two broad categories:

1. The simple interest
2. The compound interest

Simple Interest:

Let's go back to the previous example.

At the end of the period, Julie returns the money plus the interest to Mary. Soon after, however, the girl asks the same amount again to buy a new refrigerator, as the old one suddenly broke.

Marie agrees to lend the money back to her friend.

The following month, Julie firmed up her debt plus new interests, again for a total of €1,050.

Now, Marie is with her initial capital, plus €100 in interest, for a total of €1,100.

Interest is defined as simple when, once it has matured on the underlying capital, it does not generate further interest.

In our example, we note that the first €50 was not added to the capital loaned the second time.

Compound Interest:

Change of scenery.

Julie asks Marie to lend her €1,000 with the promise to return them in two years.

Mary agrees, as long as Julie accepts a compound interest on the mature borrowed capital.

In this case, Julie will not have to pay the interest immediately at the end of the 1st year but will add the € 50 interest in the capital, which in turn will accumulate 5% in the 2nd year.

At the end of the agreed period, Julie must therefore return:

1. €1,000 capital
2. €50 interest for the first year (€1,000 + 5%)
3. €52.50 interest for the second year (€1.050 + 5%)

The total capital to be returned to Mary is, therefore, € 1,102.50.

Here we have materialized € 2.50 more than the previous example, due to the compound interest.

The interest is defined as compound when, once it has matured on the underlying capital, it is added to the latter and contributes to generating further increased interest in the future.

Do you understand why the compound interest is your new best friend?

When you deposit your money in the bank account you are doing as Marie, that is, you are "lending" your money to the bank, which uses them to perform its credit function and lend it to people and businesses.

As a reward for this service, you are given an interest in the sums deposited, that is, a reward for the fact that you delay their use.

How to Take Advantage of the Compound Interest

If you do not want inflation to eat a nice slice of the real value and the purchasing power of your money, you have to make sure that the latter accrue compound interest over time.

Certainly a part of the liquidity at your disposal, you can deposit on one or more deposit accounts, or accounts with limited operations, where however higher interest rates are recognized.

For example, you could deposit your emergency fund.

The rest, however, you should invest in a portfolio of efficient financial instruments that protect your capital and create added value.

The compound interest must, therefore, be exploited for at least two reasons:

1. Increase savings while waiting for their use; and
2. Defense against inflation.

A wise thing to do is exploit the power of compound interest to make the value of your money grow faster, protecting it from loss of purchasing power.

Try to keep only small amounts on bank accounts that give you little to nothing.

You can leave just the right liquidity for your daily expenses and for the emergency fund.

Chapter 10: Seven Things to Consider When Trading Forex

It is not true that to invest in forex you have to have a lot of money, but it is true that with equal choices, a successful investment makes it proportionate to the money invested. However, the opposite is also true, that if you make a mistake with so much money, you lose more than if you make mistakes with a few. But the really important thing is that, with whatever sum you start, the stock exchange can give you earning opportunities. It all depends on how you invest. It is not an easy thing, as long as it is said, and it takes time and attention.

There are two ways to earn from the forex market:

1. Cash out the dividends distributed periodically by the currencies you have invested in; and
2. Sell your currencies at a higher price than the one you bought them.

In short, to trade in currencies and get a profit, one must know how to choose. Here are 7 things to keep in mind.

Plan the Investment

The first advice that we can give you about financial investments is about the planning of investments, or understand what the best actions to buy and diversify your portfolio are.

Even if you have never experienced this chain of events first hand, it's not a problem, because sooner or later you have to learn.

To better diversify your currency portfolio and understand where to invest, we recommend opening a demo account.

The demo account allows you not only to plan investments but also to:

- carefully analyze the stock market on which you want to invest;
- plan your investment strategies;
- familiarize yourself with the platform; and
- get familiar with the market.

If you decide to buy shares unconsciously and then open a real account and invest without the right measure, then prepare to say goodbye to your immense capital.

Of course, this is not the most appropriate and wise way to invest.

Draw the Investment Plan You Just Made

To quote W. Edwards Deming, world-renowned essayist and quality management consultant: *"If you can not describe the process of what you're doing, you do not know what you're doing."*

As for everything that requires a certain discipline, it is important to outline its investment strategy: in this way, it will be easier to articulate it. Once your strategy is written, look at it to make sure it meets your long-term investment goals.

Writing and schematizing your strategy will give you a firm base to start again in times of chaos and will make you avoid making important trading decisions dictated by emotionality. It offers you a clear outline to review and change if with time and experience you will notice defects or if you change your investment goals.

If you are a professional investor, having a written strategy in black and white will help your clients better understand the investment process you are proposing.

Learn the Difference Between Investing and Speculating

Understanding the difference between a trader and a speculator is very important. You need to know how to "use" the difference if you want to make the most out of your investments.

Before buying currencies, you have to evaluate:

- what do you want to get from the markets;
- what is your personal level of risk tolerance;
- if you are investing;
- if your goal is to speculate on the markets; and
- the time you have available to spend on investments.

If you want to get the maximum profit in a tight time, then you must have a considerable minimum time to devote to the study of markets and financial instruments. So you must understand the difference between speculator and investor.

What does a speculator do?

The speculator is that trader who buys and sells shares to make a profit in the short term; in this case, we are talking about very narrow trade times ranging from a few minutes to a few weeks.

We do not talk about years or months.

They only take advantage of the price difference between the value of the sale and purchase of the deal.

The speculator's characteristic is that it is not interested in dividends distributed by listed companies.

What does a trader do?

Contrary to the previous one, the investor, also defined as a long-term investor, invests his capital by providing liquidity to the currency pair.

In this case, the trader will buy the so-called "lots" of a given currency. The goal of a trader? Keep the stocks in his wallet for a prolonged period of time and make them profit!

This allows him to benefit from the detachment of the dividend that is added to the possible appreciation of the title.

It is very important in this case is to understand what kind of investor you are. Pay close attention to this step because it is essential to earning with investments in the forex market. Most of the trader's operating strategies are based on fundamental analysis that is very different from those of a short-term investor or speculator.

Understand the Importance of Timing (And the Impossibility of Getting It Right)

Very important is to understand when is the right time to buy and sell currencies. In this case, the timing is an indispensable part to identify the stocks to be bought.

If the correct price levels are not identified, there could very well be the risk of entering the market at a risky point. This could be unfavorable and does not allow us to quantify the transaction's risk-return ratio accurately.

Learn Your Strength as Weaknesses

Does your investment strategy follow your idea of how investments depreciate or appreciate? If so, how do you exploit your knowledge?

This question refers to your actual knowledge of the market. Ask yourself: "*What makes me smarter than the market? What is my competitive advantage?*"

You may have special knowledge of the industry or have access to a study that few others know. Or, you could get your own opinion by exploiting some market anomalies, as happens in the strategies for the purchase of securities with a low price/value ratio.

Once you have decided what your competitive advantage is, you need to decide how you can use it profitably to develop a trading plan.

Your investment plan should include rules for both purchase orders and sales orders. Also, keep in mind that competitive advantage could lose its profitability and its effectiveness if other investors begin to adopt your own investment strategy.

Or, you can be convinced that markets are totally efficient, which means that no investor will ever have a real competitive advantage.

In this case, it is better to focus on minimizing commissions and transaction costs by investing in passive instruments such as futures.

Is Your Strategy Versatile?

There is an old way of saying on Wall Street: "*The market can remain irrational longer than you can remain solven*t."

Successful investors know where their investment performance comes from and can explain the strengths and weaknesses of their strategy.

As trends and economic issues change, many investment strategies have periods of great performance followed by periods of poor performance.

Having a good understanding of the weaknesses of your investment strategy is essential for maintaining confidence in the market and investing with conviction, even if the strategy is temporarily "out of fashion".

Understand That a Good Strategy Can Be Measured

It is difficult to improve or fully understand something that can not be measured.

For this reason, you should always have a benchmark to measure the effectiveness of the investment strategy you are using. This benchmark must be consistent with investment objectives, which in turn must tune into your strategy.

There are two types: the relative benchmark and the absolute benchmark. An example of a relative benchmark could be the EURUSD pair. An example of an absolute benchmark could be a performance target.

Even if it is a time-consuming process, it is important to consider the amount of risk you are taking concerning the investment benchmark. This can be done by recording the volatility of portfolio returns and comparing it with the volatility of benchmark returns over certain time periods.

Chapter 11: Forex and Leverage

What is Leverage?

Through the use of financial leverage, a person has the possibility to buy or sell financial assets for an amount higher than the capital held and, consequently, to benefit from a higher potential return than that deriving from a direct investment in the underlying and, conversely, to expose himself to the risk of very significant losses.

How Does the Leverage Work?

Let's see how the concept of leverage works starting from a simple case.

Let's assume you have €100 available to invest in a currency pair. Let's assume that the gain or loss expectations are equal to 30%: if things go well, we will have €130. Otherwise, we will have €70. This is a simple speculation in which we bet on a particular event.

In case we decide to risk more for our investment, in addition to our €100, also another €900 borrowed, then the investment would take a different articulation because we use a leverage of 10 to 1 (we invest €1,000 having a capital initial only €100). If things go well and the stock goes up 30%, we will receive €1,300; we return the €900 borrowed with a gain of €300 on initial capital of €100. So, we get a 300% profit with a stock that only gave a 30% return. Apparently, on the €900 borrowed, we will have to pay an interest, but the general principle remains valid: the leverage makes it possible to increase the possible gains.

Considering the further case of the investment in derivatives, let's assume we buy a future that, within a month, gives the right to buy 100 grams of gold at a price set today of €5,000. We could physically buy the gold with an outlay of €5,000 and keep it waiting for the price to rise and then sell it back. If we decide instead to use derivatives, we should not have €5,000, but only the capital needed to buy the derivative. Let's say that a bank sells for €100 the derivative that allows us to buy the same 100 grams of gold in a month to €5,000. If in a month, the gold is worth €5,500, we can buy it and sell it immediately, realizing a gain of €500. With the €100 of the price of the derivative, we make a profit of €400 or 400% with €100.

This is how leverage works. Do you get the amazing power it can give to the average investor?

What Are the Potentials of Its Use?

The potential of leveraging is clear. But be careful: the leverage multiplier effect, described with the previous examples, works even if the investment goes wrong.

For example, we decide to invest €100 in our possession plus an additional sum of €900 borrowed. If the currency pair depreciated by 30%, we would remain with only €700 in hand, having to return the €900 borrowed plus interest and considering the €100 of our initial investment. We would have a loss of over €300 on an initial capital of €100. As a percentage, the loss would, therefore, be 300% against a reduction in the value of the pair of 30%.

Another element to keep in mind is that the different financial levers can be combined: in this way speculation operations are carried out using a "squared lever" with clear reflections on potential potentials.

What Are the Risks Related to Leverage?

What may appear to be an interesting tool with positive potential for the investor, on the other hand, presents risks that must, therefore, be taken into due consideration. If the financial system as a whole works with very high leverage and financial institutions lend money to each other to multiply the possible profits, the loss of an individual investor can trigger a domino effect by infecting the entire financial market.

Banks are typically entities that operate with a more or less high degree of leverage: against a certain net capital, the total assets in which the resources are invested is generally much higher. For example, a bank with equity of €100 and leverage of 20 manages assets for €2,000. A loss of 1% of the assets involves the loss of 20% of the equity capital.

The development of the market for the transfer of credit risk (from financial intermediaries to the market) has meant that the traditional bank model, called "originate-and-hold" ("create and hold": the bank that provided the loan it remains in the balance sheet until maturity), has been substituted for many operators from the "originate-to-distribute" ("create and distribute": the intermediary selects the debtors, but then transfers the loan to others, recovering the liquidity and the regulatory capital previously committed or the pure credit risk with benefits only on capital requirements), with the effect of a further increase in leverage. The spread of this second bank model is one of the factors that explain the crisis triggered on the sub-prime mortgage market.

Property price inflation has supported the issuance of loans and the exponential growth of the related market, allowing banks to make huge profits and, at the same time, increase leverage. But "the money machine" could not last long and in the end, many banks found themselves without sufficient capital to absorb the losses deriving from the inversion of the real estate market trend, resulting in fact in failed companies.

In the meantime, the example of the banks has spread within the financial system by spreading to all other financial institutions: leverage had prevailed, especially in the United States, generating a huge volume of risky investments that rested on a fraction infinitesimal of equity capital. We are thinking of the issue of so-called "credit default swaps" (derivative instruments used to hedge against the default risk of the debtor): some insurance companies were heavily exposed to the real estate market, and when the latter collapsed and the value of mortgages fell, they began to lose without having sufficient capital to absorb the losses deriving from the issue of those instruments.

In order not to risk failing and return to sufficient levels of bank capital, capital increases (not an easy task in times of crisis), the reduction of the amount of loans to businesses (granting a lower number of new loans and not renewal of those already issued) and the disposal of other liquid assets (mostly shares) can be used. The result of all this, in the period of the sub-prime crisis, was a credit freeze and a collapse of the stock market. These are the main channels through which the financial crisis has hit the real economy. Credit rationing has affected investments, and the decline in the stock market (which adds to the decline in house prices) has reduced the value of household wealth and therefore consumption.

We know that a certain level of leverage is physiological to sustain economic growth, even if we do not indicate what the optimal level is. But history teaches us how in an increasingly globalized and interdependent economic-financial system, leverage can be a trigger for speculative bubbles. And it is in these periods that the strongest disconnect between finance and the real economy is generated.

Chapter 12: Cryptocurrencies–A Different Currency Pair

One of the strategies that I am going to explain you is trading in cryptocurrency. Why do I invest mainly in crypto and blockchain-related assets? Because I truly believe they are one of the biggest revolution undergoing in this very moment and that this is the perfect time to get involved before the market explodes to the upside and prices rise at major stocks level.

Another reason that I like cryptocurrencies and their market is that they are extremely volatile and provide the average Joe the possibility to make serious money without investing a lot. It is not a secret that every time the market starts to rise, people rush into the search for the "next big win" and the question that circulates is always the same: "What will the next cryptocurrency that will go to 'the moon'?"

The issue with cryptocurrencies is that being a market that is not yet regulated in several countries, the risk of pumps and dumps, manipulation, and fraud is just around the corner. This is why I wanted to cover them in this book. Since they provide a great opportunity, I am worried that a lot of people may get involved without knowing what they are doing and will lose a lot of money down the line. Here, I want to show you what I do before investing in a particular asset and how I keep it a sustainable source of passive income.

Before getting started, here is a list of useful tools for the analysis of cryptocurrencies:

1. **Coincheckup.com** – one of my favorite sites, offers much more data than other cryptocurrency monitoring sites
2. **Coinmarketcap.com** – one of the oldest crypto price tracking sites, far more popular than Coincheckup, but offers less data
3. **Blockfolio.com** – another popular cryptocurrency tracker

Now let's get to the good stuff.

Step 1 - Understanding Your Risk Profile

Many people will advise you to buy "low capitalization" cryptocurrencies and tokens (i.e. between $10 and 100,000,000) because they have a greater opportunity for growth in terms of percentage.

Although this statement is relatively correct, you have to keep in mind that the smaller a coin is, the riskier it is to invest in it. Why? Because the project has indeed a much higher risk of failing.

In traditional investments, most people aim and are happy to get an annual return of 3% to 4%; but they could be in serious financial difficulty if the invested capital is lost, so most of the time more well-known, safer and more stable titles are selected.

Other people would instead be satisfied only with an annual yield of 7% to 12%. These people could also be willing to lose all their investment if things go wrong. In their case, they would point to a higher risk given the economic attitude they have at the base.

These two different groups of people have different "risk profiles".

It is important that in any purchase you make in your life (even for something "concrete" like a car), you do so knowingly about the financial risk profile you can afford to take.

My personal opinion is that just because something has higher chances of performance does not mean it is the best choice. In particular, I have invested mainly in the top 5 coins in terms of capitalization because they are the safest spot right now. However, I always allocate a small part of my portfolio, 10% to be precise, to low cap coins. How do I find the most promising one? Here is what I do.

Step 2 - Identification of New Coins or Tokens

There are three main ways I usually use to find the "new" coins or tokens:

1. Through the posts of the Bitcointalk.org forum, more precisely in the section "Announcements (Altcoins)";

2. In the subreddit /r/cryptocurrency; and
3. In the "Newly Added" sections of Coincheckup and "Recently Added" by Coinmarketcap.

Each of these is a great resource to discover interesting coins with great return potential over a shorter period of time. As already said, I only put in a maximum 10% of my capital into these underrated projects.

With every investment comes the possibility to get scammed and in the crypto world happens more often that I would like to see. During the last three years of experience, I have developed a series of principles that I follow to avoid being scammed. Here is what will make me decide NOT to invest in an asset.

Step 3 - Exclusion of Coins and Useless Tokens/Scams

One of the first things I do when I look at new projects is to subject them to very strict criteria to remove "fluff" projects from the list. In particular:

1. I do not buy cryptocurrencies in industries and sectors that I do not understand;
2. I do not buy cryptocurrencies whose teams are inactive in social media communication;
3. I do not buy cryptocurrencies whose start-ups/associations/companies are registered in countries where I cannot validate a solid corporate entity;
4. I do not buy cryptocurrencies if I cannot find the team members (with particular attention to the founder) on LinkedIn and validate that they are real profiles;
5. I do not buy cryptocurrencies whose teams adopt spamming strategies and do aggressive and non-informative marketing campaigns on social and non-social channels;
6. If a team is building brand new technology, I do not buy the cryptocurrency/token, unless there is a detailed technical

document explaining how it works;
7. If a cryptocurrency has a pre-ICO with a discount, I tend not to buy it. If I did, it would only be in the case where the discount compared to the public ICO is minimal and the amount purchased is "locked" for a significant period of time (to avoid massive dumps after the public ICO); and
8. I do not buy cryptocurrencies if I do not use them personally as an end user.

To help me with the process, I also use a series of questions that allow me to get more in depth and realize the true fundamental value of an asset. In particular, I really like to ask myself the following questions:

- Would I use this cryptocurrency as an end user?
- Would I pay that price as a user?
- Does this project require the development of new technology?
- What is the team's experience in this determined direction? Have they already managed a successful company? What was the performance of this company?
- Does the team have the ability to develop this technology? Are engineers and developers recognized in this sector? Do they have product managers and customer support?
- Is it clear how the project will generate users/customers?
- Why are they using the blockchain? Do they really need it or do they use the term "blockchain" to hype their project up? What are the pros and cons of using the blockchain in this case and why should the blockchain improve the current alternative on the market? (Keep in mind that currently, in most cases, blockchain-based systems are slow and expensive).

Pay attention to absolutist statements. Each project has negative aspects and consequences; a real project will be realistic in delineating them, especially the latter.

If I can see that each question has a positive answer, I will then allocate a part of my portfolio. I always invest long term, and I am willing to stay in a coin for at least one year. If for any reason I do not feel confident enough to put money into a project for at least 52 weeks, then that means that it is probably better to look at another one.

Predicting the next currency that will make the boom is impossible, out there are so many projects based on nothing that still capitalize tens of billions of dollars; in the same way, there are dozens of serious projects that deserve more, but that fails to stand out and gain visibility compared to others. The golden rule is that which applies in every financial market: diversify. By diversifying between several coins, you reduce the risk.

Chapter 13: 30 Golden Lesson to Trade like a Pro

Now that we have gone through the main mistakes a beginner makes, it is time to take a look at what we call "the 30 Golden Lessons of Trading".

1. **If you are undecided, stay still.**

It is not necessary to invest continuously. If you do not have precise ideas, it is better to do nothing and wait for clearer signs. Often, the market is full of indecision: keep calm and stack up money for the future.

1. **Cut losses and let profits run.**

This is perhaps the best known and most important rule for those investing in the stock market. An indispensable factor for the application of this rule is the identification, immediately after the purchase, of the stop loss. This is how much you are willing to lose on that investment (take into account when determining the average daily excursion of the stock). The cold and systematic application, even if painful, of the stop loss will preserve you from huge losses that would make the sale more and more traumatic, freezing capital that could be invested elsewhere.

1. **Learn from your mistakes.**

Errors are not always negative: if you follow a strategy with a method, if you apply the stop losses, you will not make particularly serious mistakes. Errors are an integral part of stock trading: you need to analyze why you made them and what you can learn from them. In this way, a small loss can become a good investment lesson for the future.

1. Take profit and invest them back.

If one of our titles is on the rise, take profit will be applied as the stock grows. A stock cannot grow indefinitely, when the trend is reversed, selling at the top, we will have had a profit avoiding further descents. If then the title should go up again, it does not matter; it will go better next time. You cannot always sell at the top since, remember, you cannot time the market.

1. Buy on the rumor and sell on the news.

When positive news on a certain title officially comes out, pay attention. It may already be too late to invest in that title since the market could already have priced it in.

1. Do not believe in "safe investments".

If someone tells you that a title will certainly reach a certain price, he either does not understand much of the stock market or is only doing his own interests.

1. Never become emotionally attached to a stock.

Some investors always follow a limited number of companies that they consider more reliable than others. There are no titles better than others, but only favorable situations and unfavorable situations. Often, instead of admitting an error, one perseveres on it with the consequence of being heavily unbalanced on a stock. This is really bad, especially if you are overcommitted to a stock in which, at that moment, the market does not believe in.

1. **Always maintain certain liquidity available.** Cyclically, we find ourselves in situations of several days of generalized decline of the whole stock exchange and often, for lack of liquidity, we can not grasp excellent buying opportunities. Keep some money aside to jump on big opportunities.

1. **Choose the right platform.**

One important rule for investing in the stock market is that the platform makes the difference. Carefully selecting safe, honest, and reliable trading platforms is the first step to make money. Those who start investing in the stock market for the first time must be careful to choose platforms that are simple to use, perhaps with high-quality educational support. Some platforms also offer add-on tools, such as notifications, social trading, and free analysis tools, to guide less experienced traders.

1. **Invest only in what you understand.**

As the "guru" of finance, Warren Buffett said, "*Never, never, invest in something that you do not understand, and above all, that you do not know*". The overwhelming majority of investors can achieve their capital growth goals by using the most common financial instruments, which are almost always simple to understand. The complex tools are best left to the great experts in the field.

1. **Diversify your portfolio.**

When investing, the word to keep in mind is "diversification." Never invest in a single title, because if that sinks, your money will come to the same end. It is always better to have diversified investments to minimize the specific risks of a company, a market, an asset class, or a currency. The more you diversify and the lower the probability of having drastic falls.

1. **Understand and evaluate the risk.**

Risk is an intrinsic component of every investment. If it does not exist, there is no return. Whether they are government bonds, stocks or mutual funds, they all have a risk component, which will obviously be greater if you want to hope for higher returns. So, if someone tells you that there is an investment without risk, it means that it is better to get advice from someone else.

1. **Look beyond direct investment.**

As an alternative to direct purchase of shares, it is possible to invest in the stock market indices through ETFs (listed mutual funds, which replicate the performance of equity and bond indices) or in mutual funds, that offer a high diversification even with minimum amounts, allowing you to invest small periodic shares (for example, €100 per month) and may even provide a monthly coupon.

1. **Do not follow the masses.**

The typical decision of who buys stocks by investing in the stock market is usually strongly influenced by the advice of acquaintances, neighbors or relatives. So, if everyone around is investing in a particular company, a beginner investor tends to do the same. But this strategy is bound to fail in the long run and it is not the right approach. There should be no need to say that you should always avoid having a herd mentality if you do not want to lose hard-earned money on the stock market. The world's biggest investor, Warren Buffett, is right when he says "Be fearful when others are greedy, and be greedy when others are fearful!"

1. **Do not try to time the market.**

One thing that Warren Buffett does not do is try to time the stock market, even if he has a very strong understanding of the key price levels of the single shares. Most investors, however, do exactly the opposite, which often causes losses of money. So, you should never try to give timing the market a chance. In reality, no one has ever succeeded in doing so successfully and consistently over multiple market cycles.

1. **Be disciplined.**

Historically, it has often happened that during periods of a high market upswing, we first caused moments of panic. Market volatility has inevitably made investors poorer, even if the market moved in the intended direction. Therefore, it is prudent to have patience and follow a disciplined investment approach as well as keeping a long-term general picture in mind.

1. **Be realistic and do not hope.**

There is nothing wrong with hoping to make the best investment, but you could be in trouble if the financial goals are not based on realistic assumptions. For example, many stocks have generated more than 50 percent of returns during the big uptrend in recent years. However, this does not mean that we can always expect the same kind of return from the stock exchange.

1. Keep your portfolio under control.

We live in a connected world. Every important event that happens anywhere in the world also has an impact on our money. So we have to monitor our portfolio and make adjustments constantly.

1. Be sure to be on the legal side of things.

If someone proposes an investment, it must be verified as an "authorized project." In our country, those who offer financial investments must be authorized by law, and this is an important safeguard for savers. The authorization is issued only in the presence of the requested requisites and, once authorized, the financial intermediaries are subject to constant supervision. Checking this is not particularly demanding: if you have internet you can even directly access the information held by the supervisory authorities; otherwise, you can contact the authorities themselves using traditional means.

1. Be skeptical and do your own research.

Nobody gives anything for nothing: be wary of investment proposals that ensure a very high return. At the promise of high returns, there are usually very high risks or, in some cases, even attempts of fraud. Be wary of "Ponzi schemes" which promise profits linked to the subsequent adhesion of other subjects, who often must be convinced by the investor himself to join. These "operations" cannot guarantee any kind of return, as they are normally supplied exclusively by the continuity of the accessions. In other words, when the new signatures are no longer sufficient to pay the "interests" to the previous subscribers, the schemes are destined to fail. Be wary of the vague and generic investment proposals, for which the methods for using the money collected are not explained in detail (what kind of securities will be purchased, at what prices, on which markets, with which risk profiles—interest rate, foreign exchange or counterparty—and whether and which hedging instruments will be used to cover such risks).

1. **Have a long-term mindset.**

According to Warren Buffett, the shares once bought, are not to be sold. It is, therefore, better to evaluate the industrial trends in the long term and then buy them, leaving aside the passengers' enthusiasm.

1. **When investing in real estate, know the area you are investing in.**

To start with, it is good that you put your focus on your area of residence or, if you live in a big city, even in your neighborhood or on one that you know well. If you think to act on a field of action too large, you risk dispersing too much energy towards something that can present totally different solutions. Dedicate yourself only to residential buildings, apartments or houses. The commercial ones, even if they can be very profitable, have other rules and in general greater difficulties. The same for the land: you can do big business, but it is not something suitable for those who start.

1. Choose the right leverage and use it to your advantage.

Real estate investments must be done with leverage. If you want to invest only with your money, then the essence of real estate investment is not clear to you. The concept of financial leverage allows you to invest with money that is not yours but to make money directly for you. Leverage an economic tool that allows you to get where you would not get only with your own strength. You can take out a mortgage (if you can afford it) or engage financial partners. It may seem strange to you but it is not at all: even the richest need partners and remember that a figure that seems almost unimaginable to you, it may be normal to somebody else.

1. "*Verba volant, scripta manent*" the Latins used to say.

So never make verbal agreements, even if it is a relative or a childhood friend. Consult a lawyer to have the templates of the documents to be used. Like everything, at first it will seem difficult, but after a few times you will become an expert in basic legal practices for the sale of real estate, and you will be able to create documents in a very short time even by yourself.

1. Consider shorter positions.

In the fixed income universe, a short duration approach is potentially able to reduce sensitivity to rising interest rates, while optimizing the returns/risk ratios.

1. **Know your risk/reward ratio.**

A higher return may be tempting, but you must be sure not to take too many risks about the remuneration you would get. In bond markets, this means avoiding lengthening duration in a context of rising interest rates. Increasing investments in riskier assets may seem appropriate at the moment when the macroeconomic scenario is quite positive, but it could turn out to be a rather risky choice if the situation should change. For example, the yields offered by high yield debt, on average 3% in Europe and 5.5% in the United States, would not be sufficient to compensate investors if insolvencies passed from their current level of 2% to a more normal one of the 5%. Conversely, market areas with a good risk/return profile, with high-rated issuers offering attractive returns, include emerging market debt, subordinated financial bonds, and hybrid corporate bonds. Aiming at long-term quality makes it possible to take on fair risks, helping to limit the impact of any adverse macroeconomic event.

1. **Take the currency pairing into account.**

Global investments are exposed to currency risks. High-yield bonds and emerging market funds, for example, are usually denominated in US dollars, but the underlying bonds they hold may be issued in another currency. Fund managers may choose to include currency risk in the overall portfolio risk as exchange rates fluctuate, or decide to contain this risk through currency hedging.

1. **Stay flexible, keep some cash aside.**

It is important to have the flexibility to underwrite and liquidate investments to seize the best opportunities. However, trades are expensive and can quickly erode earnings. This happens above all in the bond markets, given the relatively low levels of returns. The bid-ask spread is on average 30-40% of the yield, so an excess of trades erodes this margin and obviously reduces the total return. Even holding portfolios with structurally short duration, allowing short-term bonds to come to maturity naturally, can improve returns because you will effectively pay the bid-ask spread once.

1. **Build up your portfolio over time.**

If investing a small sum such as 5000 Euro, will not allow you to live on that income, it can certainly represent an opportunity, to make money. In addition, even if you have a good economic availability, the ideal is always "to take it safe," starting investing from small figures and then fuel the investment over time.

1. **The past does not equal the future.**

The story is not indicative of how an investment will result in the future and investors should always try to weigh the potential risks associated with a particular investment, as well as its possible returns.

Chapter 14: Technical Analysis and Fundamental Analysis

Technical Analysis is the study of graphs. Looking at the charts, the analyst can understand if that stock (or market) will rise or fall in a short-term, medium-term, and long-term. The Fundamental Analysis, instead, bases its forecasts on the "fundamental factors", like news, market rumors, company acquisitions, economic crises, political events, wars, etc.

Which is better between Technical Analysis and Fundamental Analysis? Who has never asked this question? The answer is simple; as always in investments, there is no better; it depends on the investor, on his way of operating in the markets, on his degree of risk, etc. In other words, there are those who are better off with one, and there are those who are better off with the other.

I personally love the Technical Analysis much more for some reasons. Let me present some of them:

- Timing: Technical Analysis offers better timing than Fundamental Analysis. Timing is "the right time to get into a position", the ideal time to enter the market. It is, in my opinion, one of the fundamental concepts to succeed in the stock exchange. If you use the right timing, you can afford a very tight Stop Loss, so you can only lose a little. So, cut the losses and let the winnings run—the golden rule of the stock exchange. Timing is obviously given by the key levels that are obtained without problems with the study of the graphs, and then through Technical Analysis.
- Flexibility: Technical Analysis is more flexible than Fundamental Analysis since it gives us key levels (for Stop Loss and Goals) in any time-frame.
- Discount: Technical Analysis discounts the Fundamental

Analysis, basic postulate of Technical Analysis. The chart already includes all the factors, all the news, all the wars, all the economic conditions, etc. As a result, if the price has risen the fundamentals will be bullish. If the price has dropped the fundamentals will be bearish. I can only take care of the chart, thus eliminating many variables.

In addition to this, Fundamental Analysis has the defect that certain news is difficult to find for a common investor, and sometimes when this news arrives, it is now useless because someone smarter than us have already used them and bought (or sold) before us.

We close with a sort of "metropolitan legend" of trading, a widespread belief (but wrong) that many still have today. Many investors believe that the Technical Analysis serves to make investments in the short term and that the Fundamental Analysis serves to make long-term investments. This is not true. Both can be used to operate in the short, medium and long-term.

So many investors will continue to appreciate one and many to appreciate the other. A good idea, sometimes, is to use both, thus combining the advantages of one with the advantages of the other. An application of this concept has been explained regarding refuge currencies and high-yield currencies in Forex.

Can Technical and Fundamental Analysis Co-Exist?

Although technical and fundamental analysis are considered as opposite poles, many market participants have made a winning combination. For example, some fundamental analysts use the tools of technical analysis to identify the best times to enter the market.

Nevertheless, many technical analysts exploit the economic fundamentals to support technical signals. For example, if a technical pattern on the chart indicates the possibility of selling, we can refer to the fundamental data to obtain a confirmation of this pattern.

A mix of technical and fundamental analysis is not well-received by the "extremists" of both schools of thought, but the benefit we can derive from fully understanding the technical and fundamental analyst's mindset is undeniable.

Chapter 15: How to Keep Improving

Once you have established a profitable trading strategy that generates a passive income every single month, you cannot fly to Thailand and live the laptop lifestyle just yet. As the millionaire, Dan Lok said, *just because it works, it does not mean it will last forever*. I really want this to sink in as it is one of the most important notions of the entire book.

When things are moving in the right direction, it is time to triple down on your effort and truly commit yourself to mastery. In particular, there are two things that I'd like you to do once the first profits start to come.

Create Partnerships with Other Traders and Start a Business

It is true that creating friendships, alliances, and partnerships is fundamental for sustainability. Having people working in your own field of interest near you can be very useful. You can exchange ideas, opinions, and advice. On the other hand, if someone thinks that this kind of alliances can be found between relatives and friends, he will find himself crashing into a wall. Friends and relatives, if not already in the sector, will be the biggest obstacle. They will be those who at every error will point their finger at you, not because they do not love you, but because the brain rejects everything that does not understand. This is why I always suggest to work on your financial goals on your own and to share what you are doing only after getting the first sign of success. Remember that at the earlier stages your mindset is very weak and even the slightest critique can make it collapse.

Find a Mentor

One of the great things about success is that it leaves footsteps: almost anything you would like to do to improve your life has already been done by someone else. It does not matter whether you are starting a business, beginning your trading journey, having a happy marriage, losing weight, quitting smoking, running a marathon or simply organizing a perfect lunch. There is certainly someone who did it very well and has left some clues.

When you can take advantage of these precious clues, you will discover that life is like a game in which you must connect the dots, and all the dots have already been identified and organized by others. All you have to do is follow their project and use their system.

Chapter 16: Choose Your Style of Trading

Now that we have spent some time talking about forex trading and how to get started on it and we did all the research, it is time to work on dealing with the actual trading styles. If the currency is a good one (which you should be able to determine from the research that you did before), it is time to pick out the strategy that you are going to use to get started. Keep in mind that if you are going with a popular stock, the price is going to be high to begin with and it can be hard to get started.

Before we look at some of the strategies that you can use with currencies trading, we need to remember that it is not a good idea to chase a stock. Chasing means that you will raise your buying price quickly because you are desperate to get the shares instead of someone else. This is a really bad thing to work with because your emotions are going to start running and you will often spend a lot more on the stock (and sometimes it will be a bad stock) than it is worth. Eventually, the buyers who chased the stock will find that the value of the stocks will go down and the price will go the same way, making it hard to sell them at all, even for a loss.

One thing that you should remember is that it is important to pick out a strategy that you want to work with and then stick with it. Most of the strategies listed below, as well as some of the others that you may find or hear about in your work, are going to help you to make a good return on investment if you learn how to use them properly and you don't skip from one strategy to another.

Some beginners find that when they make a trade and it doesn't work while using one strategy, they will try to move over to another strategy and get this one to give them some of the results that they need. They assume that there was something wrong with that initial strategy and that they just need to try something else. The problem comes when they do this over and over again, switching strategies each time that something goes wrong.

This is an example of letting the emotions get in the way of what you want to do. If you are always switching out the strategy that you want to use, you are never really learning how to use one of them, and your whole plan is going to become a mess. You need to pick one and really get to know it, understanding how it works from all angles and in all situations, to get the best results with your trading. Over time, you may find that it is better to get rid of one strategy and change it to another because the one isn't working or you find that the other one will work better with your style, but it is never a good idea to skip around on the strategies that you are using all the time because it is just going to confuse you and makes it hard to ever see the success that you want with currencies.

The good news is that when you pick a strategy to work with inside of currencies, you can avoid the issues with chasing or some of the other issues that can come up when using currencies and trying to make a purchase. There are many strategies that you can pick from so you don't have to feel that you are only going to be able to use one and not feel comfortable with it. Some of the trading strategies that you may want to consider when working with currencies include:

Day Trading

When it comes to working with day trading, the investor is going to buy and then also sell their security in just one day, sometimes doing it several times during this day with at least one of their stocks. Fortunes can be made with this kind of trading, but they can also be quickly lost. To get the day trading to work, you need to have a lot of experience and knowledge in your marketplace, a good strategy, and sufficient capital. You are not able to get into it at the last minute, and you must be able to think clearly to keep your losses in check.

There are a number of benefits of going with day trading including:

1. The potential profits that you can earn will be huge if you get more than one trade that is profitable during the day.
2. The risk that comes with the stock or company changing is going to be reduced because you are not holding onto the stocks for that long. It is not likely that the company is going to change in just a day.

There are also a few cons that come with the day trading option, which is one of the reasons that people choose to go with one of the other methods of trading. Some of the cons that you will find with day trading are as follows:

- You need to have an account balance that is pretty large before you can even get started.
- For those who are not used to working in the stock market and who can't control their emotions well can quickly lose a lot of money.
- Since you need to use a margin account, this type of trading can make you lose more money than you put in, which can be really dangerous in this option.

Momentum Trading

The next strategy that you may want to go with is momentum trading. This is a strategy that the investor would use if the stocks are moving quickly, as well as on a high volume going in one direction. When it comes to currencies, many of the investors are going to play on an upward momentum because these are not usually going to be available for a short sale.

Stocks have momentum; it is because there is some buzz that is going on around the stock, such as through the news or because of rumors. To find these stocks, you will need to do some research and read through forums, message boards, and the news to find out what is going on. You should be able to find a few stocks that are getting quite a bit of attention at a time, which means that traders are going to be playing the stock pretty hard to get the price to go one way, and then they will take their profit before it all goes downward again.

There needs to be some research that goes into using this option. You need to take the time to watch how the activity for trading on the stock is doing before you make the purchase. Ones that have the potential to be done with momentum are those that have a really high volume and stocks that are moving either much higher or in the opposite direction compared to the market. You will be able to watch out for these signs by looking at charts and watching Level 2 quotes and the price action.

So after you have a list of the stocks that you would like to use, it is time to make the purchase. You will want to purchase it as quickly as possible, at as low of a price as possible, before the momentum starts to go down again. Once you own the currencies, you need to be ready to go, watching the changes in the market, looking at charts, and seeing if there are any new filings or news. If you see that there is anything negative about the stock, such as bad news, bad indicators, or a negative trend, you should try to do a quick sell to cut the losses before moving on. This is not an industry where you wait it out to see if it gets better.

On the other hand, if the momentum keeps going up, you will still need to hold on to the stocks and wait until some of the bids start to pile up. If the momentum is going up when you receive these bids and they are high enough for you to consider, you may want to go with one of them. The momentum can quit going up at any time and could start to go lower so take a bid that you are comfortable with before the tides start to turn. There may be a chance of earning more if you hold onto them longer, but if you hold on to long, you are going to lose it all so it is better to get what you can out of them.

Some of the benefits that you will be able to see with momentum trading are as follows:

- The currencies are often going to be the ones that move the most when momentum starts to move, which means that you can make a lot of money in a short amount of time.
- You will be able to find a lot of information through message boards and other forums to pick the stocks that are right for you.

While this is a great way to make some good money in a short amount of time, there are also some cons that you will need to watch out for.

Some of the cons of using momentum trading are as follows:

- Sometimes the currencies are going to be volatile so your opportunity to sell and make a profit can be too short to earn anything.
- Companies that have dilution agendas can sometimes stall out a momentum run.
- Some people will use this idea to get more people to want their stocks. They will fake the buzz and the news, so you need

to be careful with working with them.

Swing Trading

Another option that you can work with is the swing trading. This type of trading is good if you are working on a stock that has the potential to move around in a short period. This is usually going to be for stocks that will move within the day but can go for up to four days. This is a type that will use technical analysis to look for a stock that may have momentum for their price over the short term. With this one, you are not going to be that interested in the values o the stock, but rather the trends and patterns of their price.

In a perfect market, the stocks are going to trade below or above a baseline value, or a moving average. The currencies are going to use this as both the resistance and support levels. When you are experimenting around with the charts, you will be able to see a set of moving averages will be fit to the actions of the price, and this can help out with the decisions during trading. Someone who has been in the stock market for some time would know that they should buy near the bottom of the moving average, but then they would sell before it reaches the target moving average.

There are quite a few pros that can come with this option include:

- This is a good style to use for beginners who are trying to get into the market and still makes some profits.
- Home runs are not usually going to be done with swing trading, but if you catch the beginning of a new uptrend, there is the possibility of getting large profits.
- You can use the basics of this kind of trading in any market that you would like. Big board stocks, futures, XCM, and Forex also use swing trading.

While there are quite a few positives that come with using currencies, there are also a few things that you need to watch out for. Swing trading is not an option that everyone is going to be fond of.

Some of the cons of choosing swing trading as your strategy:

- It is hard to find that perfect market where a particular currency is going to end up trading between the resistance and the support levels. This can get even harder to predict when there is a strong downtrend or a strong uptrend that are at work.
- Currencies can make it hard to time your buys the right way, especially when dealing with dilution on the stock that you purchased.

Technical Trading

Technical trading is a good option to go for when you are looking at all the points of your trading strategy. This one is going to use a Technical Analysis to help you find the right stocks that you would like to trade as well as helping you to set up your entry and then exit points to reduce losses if they would occur. Someone who picks to go with this kind of trading is going to use charts to examine the whole history of the stock, take the time to observe indicators that are going on, and then they will be able to identify the trends and patterns that are going on with the price.

There are a few different indicator groups that you can use to work with technical trading. Some of these include:

- *Strength indicators*: these are the indicators that are going to compare your current price to that of its history. This helps to show how weak or strong the stock will be. The Relative Strength Indicator is the most common one to use with this. Often it is shown at the top of your charts, and it will indicate any overbought as well as oversold price conditions. Many times this can be a tip for helping you to buy and sell at the right price for a stock.
- *Moving averages*: these are known as MA's, and they are indicators that are going to be generated by averaging out the price levels over so much time. These can help you to see how often the movements of the stock are either below or above their averages. These are known as crossovers and can sometimes indicate breakdowns and breakouts as well, something that is important to a trader who is trying to pick out what stock they would like to work with.
- *Pattern analysis*: this is the evaluation of your charts to identify price formations, such as shapes, that come up in

history. Sometimes you can see wedges, triangles, cups, handles, and more for the stock you want to work with. These formations can sometimes be used to look into the future and determine if there is going to be any downward or upward movement. Market forces often cause them, but one is showing up, whether it is natural or not, will affect the action of that stock.

- *Range analysis*: this is where you are going to use a few different things together, such as the price range and the closing and opening prices to figure out where your resistance and support levels. These can help you to figure out what the best purchase, as well as sell points, are and can tell you other information, such as the levels of a breakdown and breakout with the stock.
- *Gap analysis*: this one is going to be done when you can find gaps in the charts you are looking at. A gap is going to be a spot that is inside the chart which will be caused by a price at the opening that is higher than what it was at the close the previous period. The idea behind here is that these gaps are usually going to be filled, so you will be able to use this to figure out the buy prices since you know that the price will go back down to fill up this gap before it goes higher.

All of these options are going to need you to use analysis to figure out when to enter the market, how long to hold on to the currencies, and when to let them go to make the biggest profit possible while limiting your losses. There are many benefits of using this kind of strategy including:

- Many people are on the forums and the boards who will help you to learn how to use TA and will talk to you about how to identify these hot stocks.

- Inside of currencies, these technical moves can be pretty strong. This is because TA is all there really is to help you to judge a stock and the way that the price will move.

Of course, while many people will use this option to help them make decisions with their trading, there are a few cons that you will need to worry about. Some of these cons include:

- Bashers and pumpers can make almost all charts look like they are negative or positive, in the hopes of luring investors without experience into doing the action that they want.
- Without paying attention to some of the fundamentals, such as the news, a trade that looks good in this analysis could quickly turn around in just a few minutes and you could lose out.
- Using a technical analysis can be hard. It is complex and hard for some people to understand how to use.

Scalping

One of the other strategies that you can use when working in currencies is known as scalping. This is when the investor is going to make several trades throughout the day to make some small profits on one of the stocks that really doesn't move during that day. The scalper is going to use the bid and ask spread to make this work. They will buy their shares at the big, or somewhere close to it; they can then turn around and make a small profit. This one is not going to make them a ton of money, but it is better than nothing if you plan it out right and the market isn't moving.

You can repeat this kind of profit a few times to increase your profits. While you may only make a few dollars on each trade, when you do hundreds of these, you can make a lot of money through the day. This is sometimes considered day trading but be aware that all day trading is not scalping. Sometimes, this strategy will do well, but you need to be careful because most stocks are not going to stay constant and you may end up with one that goes down in value through the day.

There are a few benefits that come from using the scalping method in your trading strategy. The following are some of the benefits:

- For the most part, your currencies are going to have a large spread, which helps to give you a good profit.
- Currencies are sometimes going to trade sideways right after they finish with a big move or when they are trying to break through the resistance level.
- When you purchase at the bid and then sell right away at the ask, you will still get the lowest price on your purchase, and it reduces the risk when you sell as quickly as possible before things can change.

Of course, there are a few negatives that can come up from using the scalping process for your currencies. The following are some of the cons when going with this method:

- Currencies can be difficult to do this with because of their anemic volume.
- This process is going to make you work against your market makers, and this makes it difficult.
- Since currencies are high risk and this option is only going to give you a small amount of profit, it may not be the best. If you want to give it a try, it isn't bad, but some people don't think the risk is worth the reward.

All of these strategies have been used when it comes to working in currencies, and it is important to figure out which method you would like to use for your needs. You can pick any of them and see some success, but you do need to be careful. You are not going to see the good results that you want if you are skipping all over the place and not sticking with a good strategy. Those who are the most successful with currencies, as well as with some of the other investment options are the ones who will pick out one strategy and stick with it. Consider some of the strategies that we talked about in this chapter and choose the one that works the best with your needs and will help you to make the biggest profit in currencies.

No matter what strategy you use, there are best practices that all experienced and successful traders observe. These are the keys that will help you succeed. These things are not just something that you read because their true essence is in doing, so be sure to apply them to your every trade. Here are the best trading practices that you should know:

Do your research.

Do not simply focus on the currencies that you want to purchase. Keep in mind that the performance of stocks heavily depends upon the overall performance of the business. Therefore, you must also give attention to the company itself. How is the company doing in the market? Does it match up well against its competitors? Remember to research the currencies that you intend to purchase, as well as the company concerned.

The scope of research is, of course, a big task. This is one of the most important parts of trading. Also, find out the factors that affect a particular stock and understand them. Are these factors present at the current moment? Is there any chance that any of these influential factors appear in the future? If so, what are the consequences? The more research and knowledge that you have the better are your chances of investing in the right currencies.

Only invest the money you can afford to lose.

Very common advice known to all gamblers is this: "Only play with the money you can afford to lose." This is common advice given to gamblers. Although trading currencies may not be considered gambling, especially if you do not rely on pure luck, it is still similar to gambling in the sense that there is always the possibility to lose your money. Do not use the money that you need for your child's enrollment or for paying the household bills, etc. Although there is no assurance that you will lose your money, you must only invest the money that you can afford to lose. The forex market is very volatile that it is hard to guarantee that you will make a profit.

Set a limit.

It is a sound advice, especially for beginners, to decide before making any trade on a limit on how long will you continue to hold on to a losing stock, as well as for a profitable one. The forex market is extremely volatile. Although you can expect for their value to increase and decrease almost randomly, it does not always mean that a stock whose price has just decreased will soon rise.

Part of the volatility of currencies is that another big drop can still follow a significant decrease in value. Therefore, to cut down your losses, it is important to set a limit on how long would you be willing to hold on to a losing stock. In the same way, you should know how long you will hold on to a winning stock. Again, even if a stock continuously experiences an increase in value, there is still the possibility that its price can just drop dramatically, almost without any warning.

Look for patterns.

The movement of the prices of currencies can be said to be like random. The thing is, randomness creates patterns. And, if it is not random, then there is more possibility to find a pattern. If you can identify these patterns early, then you will be one step ahead. Just remember, though, that patterns are like trends; and in the world of currencies, they do not last for very long.

Observe the trends.

Analyze the graphs and tables that show the performance of certain currencies. Do not just study their current record, but also check their past performance. This is a good way for you to know if the stocks are really doing well or not. Also, do not rely completely on the latest trends. Although the latest trends can show you the most recent performances of currencies, you must take note that trends often change. In fact, in the forex market, you will barely see a trend that will last for too long.

Know the latest news.

If you are serious about trading currencies, then you should be updated on the latest news. The many factors that affect the prices of currencies are usually revealed on the news. Although the news would not state it directly, you should know that laws, businesses, economy, market behavior, and inflation, among others, can affect the prices of currencies. Take note, however, that although the news can give you valuable insights and information, what matters the most is still the actual prices of forex.

Stay calm.

Bad days do happen, and you may encounter a series of losing streaks despite doing some good research. During such a moment, or the moment when you first experience your first loss, stay calm. I repeat: stay calm. The forex market does not care about how you feel, so must remain objective and focused. If you cannot control yourself, just quickly turn off your computer or mobile phone.

Do not be greedy.

Especially for beginners, it is recommended that you stick to getting small yet regular profits. Many inexperienced traders lose their money not because of buying the wrong forex, but because of keeping the stocks for too long. Do not underestimate the high-volatile nature of the forex market. Learn to sell, cash out, and enjoy your profit.

Keep your emotion under control.

Do not be an emotional trader. Although it is good to feel passionate about trading forex, do not let your passion blind your judgment. Never make any trade when under pressure and treat trading forex as a business.

Make your own decision.

Although it is advisable to read the opinions of "experts," it is wrong to let them dictate your investment decisions. Unfortunately, many of these so-called "experts" are hacks and frauds. They promote themselves as an expert even if their overall losses outweigh their profits. Of course, there are still a few real experts out there, but even the best traders still commit mistakes from time to time. After all, the process of developing your trading strategy is a life-long journey.

Instead of relying on expert advice, you should develop your own understanding of the forex market and make your own decisions. You can compare your decisions with the pieces of advice given by "experts" and see how well you match up. Of course, you also need to check the real outcome of a particular trade to see if you have made the right investment decision.

Do not chase after your losses.

This is another advice given to gamblers. Unfortunately, although this advice is very common, many still fail to observe it. There are several ways to chase after your losses, but they all usually lead to the same unfortunate result. Usually, you chase after your losses by investing more right after you lose a trade. When you lose, you simply have this strong urge to get your money back.

Another thing people do is by continuously holding on to losing stocks, thinking that once they sell them, they would no longer save their lost investment. In any way, you are on the losing side with just a little hope of getting your losses back. The bad thing here is that you gamble your whole funds for the sake of recovering a few losses. Therefore, the risk is really high.

A good way to avoid this is by learning to accept your losses. If certain currencies fail to meet your expectations, learn to accept your losses by selling them and starting over again. When you seriously engage in trading forex, losing some investments is normal. After all, once you get lucky and hit truly profitable stocks, you will quickly recover all your losses and enjoy grand profits.

Stick to your strategy.

During the execution process, you must do your best to stick to your planned strategy; otherwise, you will not be able to measure effectiveness, as well as its full potential. Of course, there are instances that you should abandon your strategy, especially if circumstances clearly show that continuing with your strategy will result in a total loss of investment.

Only invest in currencies that have a high volume.

According to some "expert," you should only invest in stocks that trade at least a hundred thousand shares per day. This serves as a safeguard against the risk of being illiquid.

Pump your currencies.

There is a reason why the pump and dump scheme still exists despite many people being aware of such scheme: it works.

So, if you do not mind being a bit tricky, you can market yourself as an "expert" in trading currencies. You can put up a website and send out newsletters to your readers. You can then purchase cheap currencies, use your connections to gain interest in the stocks, and sell them at a premium price. If you are the type that can convince people to do what you want, then this may be an easy way for you to make money. However, if you are the type who cannot exercise a bit of trickery (which is a very good thing about you), then you can simply take advantage of people who pump and dump their stocks. How? Simply buy their currencies, preferably before they pump them or as early as possible while they pump their value. You can then wait for their price to increase, sell your currencies, and reap some profits.

Keep a journal.

Writing a journal is not required, but it is very helpful. You do not have to be a professional writer to write a journal. What is important is for you to be honest about everything that you write.

There are many things that you can write in your journal. It is also good to write your goals and reasons for why you want to trade forex. Also, write any lessons and mistakes that you have learned. It is your journal, so feel free to write about anything and everything about your trading adventure. A journal will allow you to think outside the box and be a smarter trader.

Take a break.

Trading forex has a gambling factor: It can be addicting. It is something that you can do for hours without being tired. You would feel more like playing than working. However, when you engage in research, which is a must, that is the time where you will definitely feel that trading forex involve serious work. Allow yourself to take a break from to time. Remember that you will have better mental clarity if you give yourself a chance to take a rest.

Get the latest updates quickly.

Successful traders get the latest news and respond quickly. The way to take advantage of the impact of the news on the prices of stocks is by making the appropriate trading actions just before others realize them.

For example, when you see that your currencies will soon encounter a massive drop in value, sell them right away. Also, if possible, know the news before it is even released in public. To increase the probability that certain stocks will increase in value, the stocks should also be effectively promoted. Therefore, it is helpful if you can join and be active in online groups and forums on forex trading.

Focus on the main pairs.

One of the best things about the forex market is that it is a place where you can find many start-up companies. Surely, a good number of these companies will do well. Unfortunately, some of them will perform poorly and even get bankrupt. However, if you manage to get the stocks of the good start-up companies early on, you will find yourself in a winning position.

Therefore, you must exert the effort to research and analyze the different start-up companies that participate in the forex market. When analyzing a particular company, also measure how it matches up against its competitors in the market.

Growing companies have lots of space for improvements; and as their profits increase and they continue to expand, the prices of their currencies also increase.

Have fun.

It is a common advice that you should choose a job that you enjoy. In the same way, you should enjoy trading forex. If you do not enjoy it, then maybe it is a signal that you should just invest somewhere else. Also, you can make better decisions when you are having fun.

Choose the right currencies

Always choose the right currencies to invest in. How do you know the right ones? Sufficient research. Never commence a trade without adequate research. Take note that a little research is not enough. Researches made without serious efforts are only as good as a mere toss of a coin. Also, the most profitable and attractive-looking stocks may not always be the right currencies to invest in. After all, no matter what the media says, the numbers on the forex market are what counts.

Be patient.

Patience is important when you trade currencies. Do not hurry to make a buy order simply because you have funds in your account. Also, many times, to take advantage of the high volatility of forex trading, you will have to wait for some time. Take note that every action that you make is essential. The stocks that you buy today are the stocks that you will soon sell. Be patient, wait for the proper timing, and act accordingly.

Use the high volatility to your advantage.

Although many people shy away from forex trading due to its high volatility, it is this volatile nature of forex that makes them a profitable investment. With high volatility, mastering the famous principle for making money is the key to profit: buy when the price is low, and sell when the price is high.

Chapter 17: Never Forget These Things

As a beginner, you may be a bit worried about getting started with forex trading. These are going to take a different route compared to working with traditional stock market options and sometimes it is hard to find the information that you need about the company before making the investment that you want. With that being said, it is possible to be successful when using currencies; you just need to be careful with the decisions that you make in currencies and take your time to really see the results. Some of the tips that you can follow when you get started with currencies to help you be successful include:

Ignore Some of the Success Stories

When you first get started with currencies, you are going to get a lot of information and emails about the success stories of others who have done well with currencies. These are found in social media sites and emails, but often these are unusual circumstances, or the information is all made up.

Instead of focusing on this, you need to look at the stocks on their own and see if they are going to work for you. Just ignore all of the success stories since most of these are going to be to get you to make a certain purchase. Do your research and learn about the market to determine which ones are the right ones for you.

Read Through the Disclaimers

If you are receiving a newsletter about the currencies, you need to be careful about the tips that you are reading. There is nothing wrong with picking out some of the stocks from these options, but you should be aware that most of them are sales tips and to give exposure to companies that, for the most part, are really bad and could end up making you lose a lot of money.

Most of the newsletters that you are going to pick won't give you the full story. The people who are writing them will do so to pump out the stock, and they are not going to tell you the right time to sell the stocks. They will work hard to get you to purchase their stocks, and then you never hear from them again. It is fine to read through some of these to get some information, but when the disclaimers state that these are written as a promotion for one company or another, you know that the tips are more of a sales pitch rather than as good advice.

Sell Quickly

One of the allures that you will hear about with currencies is that you can get a huge return on investment, up to 30 percent, in just a short amount of time. If you want to make a return on investment like this with currencies, you will need to sell your stocks quickly after you purchase them. Unfortunately, instead of being happy with the 30 percent or so, people will get greedy and will look to make a huge return. Considering currencies are sometimes getting pumped out and the industry is volatile, you should be happy with what you get, or you may lose out on a lot of money.

Be Careful When Listening to the Fund Management

You need to be really careful about the people you are listening to the inside of currencies trading, even when it comes to fund management of the stock currencies you are working with. These companies are trying to work to get the stocks up. When the stocks up, these companies can raise more money, and it is more likely they will stay in business. In some instances, they may not even be companies but basically insiders who are trying to get rich.

Most of the promotions that you will see come from the same group of people who will use different companies and press releases to get some hype up and make some extra money. They may have purchased the stocks at a lower price and now want to create a lot of buzz to get you to make a purchase much higher than what they paid.

In between the people who are using pump and dump (P&D) to make money and the companies who are worried about going under and want to get you to agree with them to save them from failing, it is hard to know which currencies are safe. You need to think independent of the news and some of the promotions that you hear before picking out the stocks that you want to invest in. With some good research and being critical of things you hear, it is easier to pick out the currencies that are actually good and to make the money you want.

Focus on High Volume

When you are getting started, it is best to only use stocks that have a minimum of 100,000 shares traded each day. If you go with a stock that is too low in volume, it is sometimes too hard to get yourself out of this issue. In addition, experts recommend that you pick out the stocks that are selling for over 50 cents a share. Going with stocks that are lower in price than this may seem appealing, but often these aren't considered liquid enough to really play with. But if you pick out stocks that are getting more than 100,000 shares a day traded and they are over 50 cents for each share, you are going to have more luck getting them to sell nicely.

Pick the Best Stock Out of the Bunch

You should make sure that you pick out one of the best stocks that you can find, especially when you are a beginner in this industry. Some experts recommend that you find a stock that has really good earnings overall or one that has broken out of its average 52-week highs in volume. Some of these are easy to find, but the trick with these is that you want to find ones that have these highs, but not because of a pump and dump scheme. You want the highs to be because others are interested in the stock and the value is going up naturally, not because of some buzz that is created to inflate the price.

Never Fall in Love with Just One Currency

When it comes to the forex market and with currencies, you can't fall in love with one stock. When you decide that one stock, and only one, is the option that you will go with, you are going to end up failing. You won't objectively look at the stock and this can make it hard to stick with your guns and make sure that you are thinking about profit.

There are always going to be salespeople who can come to you with a great story about their company and will make you fall in love with their product. But your job is to look at something objectively to find out if it is actually going to make you the money that is promised. With some good research and hard work, you will be able to find the right options for your needs without falling prey to others who want your money.

Do Your Research

Before you get into any of the stocks, you need to make sure that you complete your research. There is not much information that is provided inside of the currencies, although there are a few companies that will provide this information to help you out. This means that you will need to get to work and do some research. Look up the company and learn a bit about them including some press releases and other news that surrounds them. You should take a look at the market overall and see where things are going. You can even look at the current stock and see its history to learn how things are going for the company.

When you finish the right research before making a decision, you will find that it is easier than ever to get the results that you want. You will be able to make informed decisions, rather than just jumping into the mix and hoping that it all works out for the best.

Keep Your Head

If you are new to currencies trading, you may find that it is easy to get really involved with the stocks. You may get too involved, feeling that you need to keep going when you are losing money and getting too upset, or too happy, when things aren't going the way that you want. It is important to look at all of this objectively and learn how to always keep your head and think critically no matter what is going on in the market.

For those who lose their tempers quickly, those who have an addictive personality, or those who will have trouble with these almost gambling like options, it is not a good idea to get into currencies. You need to be able to take control of the situation, no matter what happens, so that you can think critically and make decisions that will help you to make the most money possible with currencies trading.

When you are first getting started with forex trading, you may be worried about how you will get to the top and start earning money with this kind of market. Follow some of these simple steps so that you can learn how to work with forex trading and get it to work for you.

Conclusion

Thank you for making it through to the end of *Forex Trading: The Ultimate Beginners Guide that shows the Secrets and the Strategies to make money trading Forex*, let's hope it was informative and able to provide you with all of the tools you need to achieve your financial goals.

The next step is to begin to apply what you have learned during the course of this book and get started right away. Our suggestion is always to open up a demo account on a broker and make a few tries before putting real money into it. Remember that you should never risk more than what you can afford to lose, so manage your capital wisely.

We hope that you find these lessons valuable and that you got the information you were looking for. Letting your money work for you will give you an incredible feeling, especially at the beginning, when you make the first gains. We are thrilled for you to start and we cannot wait to see your results coming in!

Book 2:
Options Trading

High Income Strategies for Investing

:

Understanding the Psychology of Investing, and How to Day Trade for a Living.

By: Branden Turner

Table of Contents

Introduction

Chapter 1: Understanding the Stock Market

The Stock Market
General Operation of the Stock Market
Trading Times on the Stock Exchange
History and General Knowledge
Psychological Lessons to Better Understand the Stock Market
Getting Your Feet Wet in the Stock Market

Chapter 2: Common Terms to Know Before Investing

Stock Market
Market Capitalization
Stocks
Stock Value
CFD
IPO
Bookbuilding an IPO
Mutual Funds

Chapter 3: Stock Market Research and Analysis

Fifteen Most Common Mistakes of a Beginner Investor
Relying on Emotions
Speculating, not Investing
Investing Without Planning
Thinking to be Able to Predict the Future
Not Paying Attention to Costs
Changing the Duration of the Investment "on the Go"

Not Diversifying
Doing Everything Your Broker Says
Not Reading Prospectuses and Contracts Well
Buying Unit-Linked (and Index-Linked) Policies
Buying Bonds From your Bank
Believing to Get Rich with Online Trading
Listening to Economists, Politicians, and Mass Media
Wanting to Become Successful Overnight
Not Taking Profits

Chapter 4: How to Pick a Trading Service and a Broker

Buy Shares to Become Shareholders
Buy and Sell Shares with Online Banks
"How much does the purchase or sale of the shares cost?"
"What shares can be bought or sold online?"

Chapter 5: Ways to Trade

Stocks vs. Other Investments
Leverage — The Huge Advantage of Stock Investing
Earning Potential
Penny Stocks
The Risks
The Benefits

Chapter 6: When to Buy and Sell

Invest in Stocks
Capitalization of Companies
Return over Equity (RoE)
Price/Earnings Ratio
Price/Value Ratio
Dividend Yield

Rating and Target Price

Chapter 7: Long-Term Investing vs. Day Trading

"Which is better?"
"What is the difference between trading and saving?"
"Who should save?"
"When is the time to trade?"
"What does trading wisely mean?"

Chapter 8: Predicting the Market

Features of a Good Chart
"What is chart analysis?"
Most Used Graphs for Graphic Analysis
Wedge
Pennant
Flag
Rectangle
Support and Resistance
Triangle
Broadening
Diamond
Rounding and Spike
Double Top and Double Bottom
Triple Top and Triple Bottom

Chapter 9: Diversification and Managing Your Portfolio
Chapter 10: Swing Trading Options
Chapter 11: Things to Ponder Before Entering the Market

Easy Money is Like Santa Claus: "It does not exist!"
Gold and Cash do not Give Interest
The Recipe for a Winning Strategy

Establish Investment Goals
Establish the Degree of Risk Tolerance
Studying
Choose the Long Term
Monitoring
Use the Leverage
"You do not need to be a finance guru to invest in the stock market!"

Conclusion

Introduction

Congratulations on downloading *"Options Trading,"* and thank you for doing so.

The world of options trading is growing increasingly chaotic, and downloading this book is the first step you can take towards actually doing something about it. The first step is also always the easiest. However, the information you find in the following chapters is so important to take to heart as they are not concepts that can be put into action immediately. If you file them away for when they are really needed, then when the time comes that you actually use them, you will be glad you did.

To that end, the following chapters will discuss the primary preparedness principals that you will need to consider if you ever hope to really be successful in the investing world. This means you will want to consider the quality of your options—including the potential issues raised by their current value, how they can be best utilized in an emergency case to drive in quick cash, and how to operate with them properly.

With stock selection out of the way, you will then learn everything you need to know about trading in a wide variety of markets including stocks, forex, and commodities (using the options instrument in each market). Rounding out the three primary requirements for successful options trading, you will then learn about crucial risk management principles and what they will mean for you. Finally, you will learn how investing is the quickest way to reach financial freedom.

There are plenty of books on this subject on the market, thanks again for choosing this one! Every effort was made to ensure it is full of as much useful information as possible, so please enjoy!

Chapter 1: Understanding the Stock Market

Let's start this book by taking a look at the dynamics of what we will be the foundation of our discussion: the stock market. When we are talking about swing trading with options, in fact, we implicitly refer to the stock exchange. Therefore, having a clear understanding of what goes on in this market, is the first step to become a successful trader.

Everyone or almost everyone has already heard of the stock exchange or its most popular assets, such as the MIB 30 and other indexes or shares of major global companies.

But few among the non-professionals really know the meaning of these often-technical terms and that they are (wrongly) considered reserved for the most aggressive traders.

In fact, the Exchange is a market accessible to everyone, whether through banking products, such as securities accounts, accumulation plans, or through an online trading platform.

The Stock Market

Contrary to what one might think, the history of the stock exchange is quite old, even though its concept has largely evolved over time. Indeed, the stock exchange made its appearance in the fourteenth century in Brussels, Belgium.

Today, even if the stock market is always a place of exchange, it is first and foremost a large market in which financial securities are exchanged. These financial securities may relate to the shares of large companies, bonds, currencies or even commodities such as gold or oil.

However, in this case, it is not a matter of exchanging physical products or merchandise, but only of securities that represent a certain evolutionary value.

General Operation of the Stock Market

Stocks could, therefore, be defined as a market in which buyers and sellers meet. But, unlike the traditional market, it is not the sellers who decide the price of their securities but the buyers.

It is then the order book that accounts for the prices decided in this way.

Ultimately, the more the securities of a stock market are required by the buyers, the higher the price goes up. On the contrary, when demand is weaker, their price falls.

The stock market on which securities can be traded is also called the "primary market." It is therefore on this market that companies can issue what are called "shares," that are then bought by investors, private individuals or professionals.

Thanks to these purchases of securities, companies can obtain the money necessary to make investments.

But the shares are not the only assets traded on this market since there can also be bonds or financial securities.

Investors' interest is speculative given that they buy a security at a price considered lower than the price that could subsequently reach for a gain or receive what are called "dividends" according to the economic performance of the issuing company of these securities becoming "shareholders."

Thanks to this system of securities and the advent of new technologies, the stock market has strongly developed on an international scale. Today there are almost as many stock exchanges as there are capitalist countries, although in most cases this market is virtual and does not include physical "trading rooms," the latter replaced by complex computer networks.

To better understand the importance of the stock exchange, know that in the single financial center of Milan, billions of euros are exchanged every day.

Trading Times on the Stock Exchange

Maybe you do not know it but trading on the stock exchange offers the possibility of dealing online continuously or 24 hours a day, thanks to the overlapping of the opening hours of the different international stock markets. In fact, the world's big financial centers are eight and their trading hours are listed in three major sessions: the Asian session, the European session, and the North American session.

But we must also consider the legal and solar hours that are not the same depending on the time zone. Let's take a look at the most important time zones for the stock market.

The Asian session

At the beginning of the week, the Asian session is the first one to open. This session includes the stock exchange centers of Japan, China, Australia, New Zealand, and Russia as well as other smaller centers. Asian assets and currency pairs including currencies of these countries are therefore the most volatile in these times. The same applies to economic publications.

The trading hours of the Asian session are as follows:

- Opening hours of the Asian market: at 4 in summer and 3 in winter
- The closing time of the Asian market: at 8 in summer and 7 in winter

The European session

The European session is obviously the most interesting for European investors. It is the second to open after the Asian session and also regroups several major stock exchanges including Italy, France, Germany, Switzerland or the United Kingdom. It should be noted that London's financial center is the largest in the world and more than 30% of financial transactions are carried out in this center every day. Trading volumes are therefore very high during the European session and therefore involve extremely volatile and interesting movements in terms of trading.

The trading hours of the European session are as follows:

- European market opening hours: 12.00 in the summer and 12.00 in the winter
- The closing time of the European market: at 16 in summer and at 17 in winter

The North American session

Finally comes the North American session, which is, therefore, the last to open and close the market cycle. Obviously, this session is also one of the most followed by traders all over the world because it is during this period that US assets are traded. This session includes the financial markets of the United States but also of Canada, Mexico and the countries of South America. It is on the stock market in New York that the volatility is higher at this time of day.

The trading hours of the North American session are as follows:

- Opening time of the North American market: at 17 in summer and at 17 in winter
- The closing time of the North American market: at 21 in summer and at 22 in winter

History and General Knowledge

The Stock Exchange is the market where sellers and buyers can trade values, foreign currencies, services, and goods. The stock exchange thus becomes an important place to put companies in touch, looking for resources to support their production and investors.

Already in the Middle Ages, the scholarship gathered merchants and notaries who dedicated themselves to mercantile and financial activities.

In the twelfth century, Venice became the main Italian square; here were introduced some innovations later adopted by other cities such as the negotiation of the public debt and the turn of the bill.

Bruges, in West Flanders, is the first European city to have a physical place for exchange, where the sale takes place according to new stock exchange rules. The industrial revolution leads to the birth of the modern stock exchange in Italy, following the example of Bruges (Trieste, Rome, Milan, Florence, Naples, Turin, Genoa, Bologna, Palermo, and Venice).

We can distinguish two types of market-based on the services and products exchanged:

1. the stock exchange;
2. the commodities exchange.

The Stock Exchange is the market in which financial instruments already in circulation are exchanged, such as bonds, shares, futures, warrants, etc.; as a consequence, the stock exchange is a secondary market (in the primary markets, investors buy the goods as soon as they reach the market).

In the commodities exchange, the sale involves goods of different types, placed in appropriate warehouses. Here buyers and sellers can exchange the deposit policies, which guarantee the presence of the goods and the right of withdrawal.

The sale and purchase of outstanding securities are regulated by precise rules; once the system of the on-call auction was over, where the agents exchanged paper documents, the market takes place via an electronic circuit where it is also possible to exchange government bonds and bonds.

Among the main types of shares, we distinguish the ordinary ones, as they assign precise administrative and financial rights to the holder (right to vote in the meetings, to request assembly, liquidation, option, etc.).

Preferred stock (preferred shares) guarantee special property rights to the owners; in the event of dissolution of the company, for example, "privileges" are granted in the distribution of profits (as provided for in the company by-laws).

Savings shares grant ownership rights to assets; however, they exclude administrative rights, including the right to vote.

Poster-gate shares provide for limitations in both administrative and patrimonial rights (generally excluding voting rights).

Limited-voting shares include special restrictions on administrative rights, such as voting limited to certain topics; according to American law, they must guarantee property privileges to the owner.

As previously mentioned, the financial market is structured in financial centers, where various financial services are treated.

The largest financial center is in New York, where the Nyse is located (the New York Stock Exchange all commodities), the Nasdaq (technology stocks), and the Amex (the American Stock Exchange collects many small capitalization companies that sell securities of various kinds).

Other important financial centers include Tokyo and London (the most important in Europe).

Psychological Lessons to Better Understand the Stock Market

Because of the continuous ups and downs that have involved international stock exchanges in recent months, many have begun to ask themselves the fateful question: "Is investing in shares still the best strategy to multiply my savings?"

The financial markets, in general, can be an extraordinary opportunity: not only stocks but also cryptocurrencies or forex can give great satisfaction even if, however, it is necessary to have preparation before going into rash choices.

Let me ask you a question: how much did you study or work to achieve the experience you have in your current job? I imagine we are talking about several years and still thousands of hours of study and practice.

Trading is no different. When trading, you compete on a par with people who do it by profession: you must, therefore, have humility, work, perseverance, intelligence, and method. If you really apply, in a few months you can decide to give up your job because you can earn a lot of money with something that requires commitment and constancy, but without being stressed or having to spend all day on the trading sites.

Getting Your Feet Wet in the Stock Market

Are you looking for safe and profitable investments? Finding solutions of this type is not easy, and you know very well. That's why you decided to take the smartphone, the PC or the tablet to deepen.

In this part of the book, we have decided to provide you with 3 concrete solutions to invest immediately, without making endless queues in the bank and without losing control of what you do.

The strategies that we suggest are ordered according to the risk profile, so we start from the less risky ones to get to the more aggressive ones.

We have written it in several books of this series, we underline it here too for safety: there are no safe investments and at the same time with double-digit returns. The times of government bonds and generous postal coupons have long since come to a close, the current economic situation sees interest at historic lows owing to the ECB's maneuvers in recent years.

In summary:

Few risks = Few Earnings

Many Risks = Potentially Increased Earnings but High Chances for Huge Losses

We come now to the merit of our discussion, here are the best solutions for investing that we have chosen for you.

Santander Consumer Bank is the most remunerative deposit account

Are you looking for a 100% capital guarantee? The deposit account is the best solution even if, in light of the considerations made before, you do not have to expect double-digit returns.

The best deposit account of the moment is that of Santander Consumer Bank which offers you an annual 1.8% on deposits at 36 months.

The advantages of Santander's offer can be summarized as follows:

1. 100% security;
2. Open it online: no stress, if you are from a PC, you just need to fill out a form (you can do the same thing if you are on a smartphone) and just leave a few data. The procedure will be completed by phone at the time you indicated;
3. No penalty in case of early release: if you withdraw money before the scheduled time, you lose nothing;
4. 0 Opening costs and management fees: you do not have to pay anything to make money.

To all this, we must add that Santander also provides the unconstrained option that allows you to receive 0.5% per year on free sums. This option can be mixed with the tied one: for example, out of 30 thousand euros, 20 thousand can be tied up at an interest rate of 1.8%, while the remaining 10 thousand free ones receive 0.5%.

Santander is a solid institution, active throughout the world with 122 million customers and over 160 years of history and is now the best solution for those looking for a deposit account free of risks and concerns.

MoneyFarm: the tech alternative to depositing accounts

MoneyFarm is an American start-up that has created a convenient platform to invest online: it is easy to understand and is safe, as we have also explained it in our review.

You can earn up to 5.41%.

The bank deposit accounts, at this stage, have returns that only in a few cases exceed 1.5%. If you're looking for granitic safety, go back to paragraph 1 where we talk about Santander.

However, if you are looking for better profitability at the same risk, you should pay attention to what you are reading. MoneyFarm, in fact, is an alternative to deposit accounts because it offers balanced investments with an almost similar degree of risk.

By signing up for MoneyFarm, you have the following advantages:

- Personal assistance of a team of competent advisors;
- Choose where to invest by filling in the questionnaire in which you indicate your degree of risk;
- You can start testing the goodness of the platform even with a small capital: just $ 500 is enough to try.

With MoneyFarm you can plan your investments and earn up to 5.41% per year, choosing the composition of your portfolio based on your risk profile. MoneyFarm aims to invest in funds with lower operating costs and to guarantee maximum transparency to customers.

You can start investing immediately even at $ 500. Before choosing the strategy, the team of experts helps you to plan your goals exactly.

Registration is free: it takes 3 minutes to start to know it, you can also try it on a smartphone as it is really very easy to use.

Unlike many structured platforms for high-risk investments (think of trading or options), MoneyFarm allows you to operate even if you have a low-risk appetite and is undoubtedly a real alternative to deposit accounts or other banking products that make a lot less.

The portfolios are constantly monitored by a team of experts, and free assistance is guaranteed for the entire duration of the relationship.

It is possible to use the live chat service or to set up a telephone appointment thanks to a special toll-free number. The seriousness is certified by the prizes and awards obtained by leading international financial experts and opinions on the web that are definitely positive. You also choose how much you are willing to risk, and the staff helps you plan the route step by step.

Social Trading

Compared to the previous solution, we are facing a decidedly riskier way: let's underline it immediately, to avoid misunderstandings. If the world of finance interests you, keep reading because you found what you were looking for.

Have you ever tried to approach online trading? If you did and you gave up, most likely you came across the difficulties of a world where only the professional traders, that is, have experience, years of study and time to constantly monitor what is going on. happening in the market in which they operate.

The social trading we want to talk about is precisely created to solve this gap in skills between professional and non-professional investors. eToro, the first social trading platform, allows you to make copy trading: you can, in other words, copy the winning strategies of top traders emulating their successes.

The principle is simple: by investing as the best, you earn like the best.

How does eToro work?

eToro allows its members to copy the strategies of the best American and world traders, called popular investors. Top traders are certified and chosen among the best that invest through the platform.

In particular, you can order them and select the ones that interest you the most according to two criteria:

1. **Earnings** - Simple: see who made the most money in a given period (6 months, 12 months, 24 months) and copy from those who have achieved gains of 25%;
2. **Risks** - If you want to adopt a more conservative strategy, you only need to copy from traders who say they risk less, to limit your exposure to losses.

With eToro it is possible to invest in the following markets:

- stocks;
- forex;
- criptovalute;
- commodities;
- CFD.

Of course, copying from the best does not completely eliminate the risks because past earnings are not a guarantee for the future. You will agree, however, that when you decide to dedicate yourself to finance, the risk is part of the game, and with social trading, you have the opportunity to take it down in the initial phase and learn from the best.

There are already 4.5 million investors who have relied on social trading to invest like the best: if finance fascinates you and you do not think you have a great experience, eToro is the most effective solution to start investing.

To start, you only need to:

- Create an eToro account;
- Choose the trader to copy from, taking care to select one with a strategy similar to your goals;
- Deciding how much to invest: $ 190 is enough to start copying from the best ones.

eToro is a win-win system designed to share knowledge and earnings and is the best way to debut on the stock market.

Chapter 2: Common Terms to Know Before Investing

Before getting started, it is important to learn the basic terms and how they are used by the experts. In this chapter, you will find a simplified dictionary with the most popular words related to the investing niche.

Stock Market

The stock market is the digital place where the largest number of transactions involving the shares, i.e., the shares of corporate capital, takes place.

In Italy, for example, the stock market is called MTA - Electronic Stock Market - and it should be noted that it does not coincide with the famous "Borsa di Piazza Affari" but represents one of the most important segments.

In fact, at "Piazza Affari," different types of financial instruments are traded, and the market is divided according to the type of contracts traded in:

1. MTA, the electronic stock market;
2. SEDEX, the segment in which instruments such as covered warrants and certificates are traded;
3. MOT, the electronic bond market in which bonds like (except for those convertible into shares), government bonds, Eurobonds and ABS, i.e., securities deriving from the security of loans are traded;
4. TAH, after hours, the electronic market in which it is possible to negotiate after the closing of the Exchange, but only for the instruments of the MTA (shares) and the SEDEX (covered warrants and certificates);

5. ETFplus, the electronic market in which UCITS units or shares are traded (SGRs and Sicavs);
6. IDEM, the market for derivative instruments (futures and option contracts on currencies, interest rates, and financial instruments). Exceptions are forwarders that are derivative contracts traded on OTC markets, over the counter, that is not regulated.

Market Capitalization

The stock market is also divided into sections by the capitalization threshold.

What, however, is the market capitalization?

The size of a listed company is measured in capitalization, that is, the value given by the number of shares available for that company multiplied by their market price.

The sections in which common markets are divided are:

- Blue chip, where the shares of the 40 largest companies are traded (over 1000 million euros);
- Mid Cap, where the securities of the 60 listed companies with high capitalization are traded but which do not fall among the Blue chips;
- Small Cap, where the shares of companies that do not fall between the Blue chips or the Mid Cap are bought or sold;
- Micro Cap, for companies that do not fall within the minimum liquidity criteria necessary for the other segments;
- Star, for companies with a capitalization of between 40 and 1,000 million euro, but with high transparency, governance and liquidity requirements;
- MTA International where the shares of companies listed on EU exchanges are traded.

Stocks

The stocks are portions in the shared capital of companies, incorporated in joint-stock companies. The two main types of stocks are:

- **Ordinary Stocks** - are those held by the shareholders of a company. They hold voting rights in corporate assemblies and profits deriving from dividends and capital gains;
- **Savings Stocks** - shares of this type do not have voting rights, but they guarantee patrimonial privileges such as dividends, i.e., the distribution of profits. They are mainly intended for small investors.

Stock Value

Each share of each company is traded or bought or sold on a price basis: the market value. This price evolves continuously by the number and the sign of the contracts concluded.

For example, if you read that the Enel stock is up today, it means that many investors are buying Enel shares.

For the classical laws of economic demand and supply, if the demand rises, the price also rises. At the end of the day, when the session is officially closed, the official price of the Enel share will be obtained in this case, by the result of all the fluctuations that the value of the stock suffered during the session based on the number of exchanges it is traded on.

What drives an investor to buy the shares of a company at that particular moment? As we have already said, the formation of share prices is a dynamic process like any other commodity market.

The value of a company stock affects:

1. Corporate performance (the state of health of the company, the size of its assets, future growth prospects, ownership

structures, extraordinary finance transactions such as acquisitions, mergers and demergers): the improvement in performance is matched by an increase in price and investor's propensity to buy those shares; vice versa, the opposite happens, that is, depreciation. Who owns those shares will sell them, increase the bid and drop the price in question;
2. performance of the sector, or the performance at the same time as other companies belonging to the same sector, also on other global stock exchanges;
3. macro or foreign policy data directly or indirectly relevant to a company: positive news generate purchases and appreciation, negative news push sales and the depreciation of the stock;
4. news or rumors about the company, such as the discovery of new deposits for companies in the oil sector, or the registration of a new patent for a company in the pharmaceutical sector or news about possible mergers, joint ventures or acquisitions.

CFD

This is a key point that actually explains why there is much less bureaucracy for forex trading than for buying and selling bank shares. CFDs (Contract for Difference) are contracts for differences that follow the performance of a given underlying (share, currency, index, etc.) and that can be exchanged, that is, bought or sold. CFDs differ from shares because they are not co-owned by a company and therefore do not give voting rights to those holding them. However, CFDs offer the same economic benefits as equities, such as profits, dividends, and splits.

In even more technical terms, the CFD exchanges the difference in value between the opening price of the certain underlying security (e.g., share) and its closing price. Following this mechanism, the trader who negotiates CFDs:

- Gets a positive result if it buys before the underlying goes up
- Gets a negative result if it sells before the underlying goes down

The mechanism is very simple, and we are sure that it is already clear. We need to buy if we think that a stock is close to the upside, we need to sell it if we think that a stock is close to the downside. CFDs follow the values of the underlying assets so you can get positive results just like shareholders, but playing at home from the comfort of your home.

IPO

A good definition of IPO is that the Initial Public Offering is an instrument governed by the law through which a company obtains the dissemination of its titles among the public. Using what is technically called the creation of the float, the company obtains the listing of its securities on the regulated market.

Said in these terms may seem difficult. For those who are just beginners, we can say that the IPO is a solicitation to invest. Thus, the Initial Public Offering is a real invitation to invest. Having clarified the meaning of IPO let's move on.

How does the Initial Public Offer work? The legislative background of this application is represented by the Consolidated Law on Finance (Legislative Decree 58/1998). This law provides for a whole series of provisions on information and transparency. The indistinct public of the subjects potentially interested in the IPO (recipients of the offer) has the right to know all the useful information to decide whether to join the IPO in full awareness.

The IPO process is decidedly long and complex. By regulation, the IPO foresees the involvement of a series of very different subjects. The following subjects participate in the various phases of the Initial Public Offering:

- the issuing company
- the global coordinator
- the sponsor
- the specialist
- the financial advisor
- the law firms in charge
- the members of the placement consortium

When one wonders how the IPO works, it should be noted that the first phase of the process is represented by the sending to SEC of the prior communication from the company concerned. The prior communication is an official document that the company presents to SEC. The same company that aims to be listed on the stock exchange is responsible for drawing up the Prospectus according to the legal framework.

From what we have said, it is easy to deduce that an IPO can last even a month. If you consider the whole procedure for admission to the stock market, then you also get to 4 or even 6 months. In short, before betting on the performance of a listed, must pass quite a bit of time. The long times, of course, also impact on the possibility of trading CFD on the shares of that listed company.

Bookbuilding an IPO

When referring to this method for fixing the price of the offer on the stock exchange, the first question concerns the definition of bookbuilding. With this strange term, we indicate the process by which the application form of the institutional investors who have submitted an order concerning a security offer transaction is drafted. Through this process, the price of the same securities is set.

The IPO bookbuilding provides for the formation of the price range through the demand expressed by the institutional investors themselves.

The global coordinator manages this process. This figure has the task of collecting all the purchase/subscription orders of institutional investors in a book called the institutional book. Orders are collected based on price or time priority or size. Each order can be expressed in the number of shares or in counter value. Finally, each order is linked to the price limit indicated by the originator. Through this process, it is possible to draw a curve which shows the price of the IPO.

Mutual funds are financial institutes whose purpose is to invest the funds raised by savers. The aim is to create value, through the management of a series of assets, for the fund managers and for the investors who have invested in it.

Three main components characterize a mutual fund (later simply fund):

1. The fund's participants are the investors who invest in the fund's assets, acquiring shares through their capital
2. The management company, which is the management hub of the fund's activities, which has the function of starting the fund itself, of establishing its own regulation and managing its portfolio
3. Depositary banks which physically hold the fund's securities and keep cash in hand. The banks also have a controlling role on the legitimacy of the fund's assets by the provisions of the Bank of America and the fund regulations.

The costs incurred by those who enter into a mutual fund are the following:

- The entry or subscription commission paid at the time of the first payment. It is generally inversely proportional to the size of its investment (the more you invest, the less you pay) and it is higher for the so-called equity funds than for the balanced ones. There are also funds that do not provide for an entry fee:

they are the so-called no-load funds
- The management fee, on the other hand, is the cost borne by the cross-party fund manager. It is calculated on an annual basis but generally paid on a semi-annually, quarterly, or monthly basis.
- The extra-commission of performance is instead an optional commission that some self-financing funds to reward if, thanks to their ability, the fund's return exceeds a certain threshold based on pre-established parameters.

Mutual Funds

The unit value of each individual share of the various funds is published daily in the newspapers. On the NASDAQ website, it is also possible to follow the price trend of the shares of the various funds in exactly the same way that the trend of the shares is followed. The prices in question already incorporate the return on the fund.

There are various types of mutual funds, the best known are the following three:

1. Equity funds invest mainly in shares or convertible bonds. They are generally riskier but tend to guarantee higher returns and, in any case, guarantee lower fluctuations than simple equity securities as they generally balance their share with non-equity investments such as ordinary bonds, government securities and with the liquidity held. Another way in which risk balancing is generally achieved is to differentiate by geographical area and therefore also by evaluating the fund's investments.
2. Bond funds, these are funds that invest mainly in ordinary bonds and government bonds: this type of funds generally has the advantage of being less risky, but the disadvantage of being less profitable

3. Balanced funds are funds that aim to balance the various forms of investment to obtain performance and risk profiles initiated between those of equity and bond funds.

Chapter 3: Stock Market Research and Analysis

Markets in recent times have become more complex, but also more volatile.

In simple words, the risk is increased. Economic factors, central bank interventions, negative rates, low inflation, and algorithms are changing the equity, currency, and commodity markets.

It seems that you no longer look at the fundamentals, but you buy the title of the moment and the one that presents a lower risk (or, to say it better, people think it presents a lower risk). In such difficult markets, small investors who invest in the stock market do not have an easy life. But this does not mean that they have to abandon the shares: with hard work and perseverance, everyone can become a skilled investor.

Fifteen Most Common Mistakes of a Beginner Investor

To help you start your journey, we have collected 15 of the most common mistakes beginner investors make. If you are able to avoid them, you will be one step ahead of the competition and will better understand how to analyze the market.

Relying on Emotions

Most people lose on the stock market because they cannot manage their emotions.

It is proven that small savers buy in the upward phase of the markets, and panic sells at the first sign of decrease. Then what happens is that the market recovers and they are now out.

This happens because of the poor financial education of the average American investor.

One who does not know how to assess the risk does not know the diversification and cannot select the securities to put in the portfolio. He does not know how to calculate the average value of an asset.

He does not even know how to use a spreadsheet to calculate the volatility of a stock.

And it is precisely the lack of ability to manage the risk that will make him make bad decisions and will ultimately result in a loss.

Speculating, not Investing

Another mistake that many often make is to confuse speculating with investing.

If you invest for the very short term, you increase the risk, and it is not a question of investment but of speculation. Knowing how to define investment speculation is essential.

Before entering a title, you must define your time horizon and consider where to put the stop loss. One classical example of speculation is "binary options." They are often promoted as an investment, but they are not. For those who do not know what they are, binary options are bets placed on the price of an asset in the next 30 seconds. Yes, you read that right. Seriously, stay away from them.

Investing Without Planning

On the stock market, invested capital should not be necessary for daily life.

Before investing, plan these goals. Someone invests because in the future he wants to buy a bigger house. Others may invest for when they retire, but also for a holiday.

There are those who do it for their children. The real question is: why are you investing?

Thinking to be Able to Predict the Future

What do Warren Buffet from Omaha and life coach Tony Robbins have in common? Both agree on the big risk that comes when our money is at stake.

During an interview with CNBC, Tony Robbins warned against a big mistake that is committed when it comes to investing for the future, which is, trying to predict the ups and downs of the market.

No one can predict the future, says Robbins, and legendary investors like billionaire Warren Buffett and the founder of the titanic hedge fund Bridgewater Associates, Ray Dalio, tend to agree.

"Your plan for the future cannot be based on trying to time the market because you're going the wrong way."

Instead of buying and selling shares based on how the small change, Robbins suggests thinking long-term.

"You cannot afford to try and time the market. What we must do is study the long-term elements and have a diversification plan that protects when we are wrong."

Buffett is also an important supporter of this type of strategy called "buy and hold," so much so that he wagered that the S & P 500 stock index would surpass hedge funds (which actively change investments). Now, it seems that most likely he will win that bet, which will bring him an extra $ 2 million in prize money.

Robbins also relies on the advice of Dalio, who founded the largest hedge fund in the world, Bridgewater Associates, which has difficulty identifying the right times to get in and out of investments. So, for Robbins, the best idea remains to look long-term, and both he and Buffett suggest that they consider investing in low-cost index funds the best thing to do.

Not Paying Attention to Costs

We have said it in all languages: costs can kill you financially. Investing € 15,000 for 30 years can result in € 106,000 capital if made with an ETF or a low-cost mutual fund, and € 67,000 if it is carried out with a mutual fund that has 2% of TER. See for yourself.

Realistically, saving costs is the only true "free money" that you can get as an investor. Financial products with high commissions are more often than not skylarks, just think of how overestimated Alfa management's idea is.

Changing the Duration of the Investment "on the Go"

It usually works like this: you have chosen a portfolio assuming a certain duration of the investment, then the market "coughs," an instrument within the portfolio loses 5-6%, you read some negative opinions about it, start to shake like a rabbit and eventually sell. This change of time horizon does monstrous damages: typically, it makes you lose about half of the gains. Solution: invest a little at a time and do not think about it anymore.

Not Diversifying

Diversification is useless only if you are able to predict the future and know what the best investment will be. If instead (as a normal human being) you do not have paranormal divinatory skills, you should diversify your portfolio a little. But without exaggerating (more on that later).

Doing Everything Your Broker Says

If the bank, the promoter or the broker push a product, run to check the costs: in 9 out of 10 cases it is the most convenient product for them and, as you can guess, the most expensive for you.

Not Reading Prospectuses and Contracts Well

By law, intermediaries are forced to write everything they do in a "contract" type of document. Often times, they will do it with that legal language that sends you into narcosis already in the second line. But you have to read everything if you do not want bad surprises. Remember that you are responsible for your money and should not put the blame on others.

Buying Unit-Linked (and Index-Linked) Policies

These policies are among the less transparent financial products that can be found, are padded with high commissions in favor of those who sell them. The seller will tell you a lot of nice stories about the capital guarantee. Beyond the fantasies, with a unit-linked (or index-linked) policy, in 90% of cases you will have an expensive product, with severe penalties in case of early disinvestment and, after 10 or 20 years of payments, you will typically be rewarded with a disappointing performance (but, if you can console yourself, you will have made the man who sold it to you very happy).

Buying Bonds From your Bank

Bank bonds usually make less of a BTP of the same maturity, because they bear implicit charges, i.e., costs. Then, they are on average riskier and less liquid. And this is even more true for subordinated bank bonds, whose holders, with the recent entry into force of the bail-in, are likely to be called to put their hands in the portfolio in the event of the issuer's default. Before buying these bonds, study them carefully, compare them with a governmental or supranational title (like BEI, BIS, etc.) and only then decide.

Believing to Get Rich with Online Trading

The colorful world of online trading is teeming with gurus to convince you that you will become rich thanks to their fabulous courses or their financial market forecasting site. Know that succeeding with trading is very difficult: in the vast majority of cases you will end up losing money and time. Learn to save and invest, not to trade.

Listening to Economists, Politicians, and Mass Media

The noise in the ears distracts: eliminate it. So here is, for you and only for you, our personal list of noises that you have to get rid of.

Economists

Think about how little they have put us right in the story: for example, in 2009 they did not recognize the worst crisis since the Great Depression of 1929, in spite of a myriad of signals and, above all, the fact that the recession was already under its way.

Politicians

Except for rare exceptions, the events of any Parliament are lively, full of funny and quarrelsome characters that combine all the colors, going from crisis to immediate solutions, and then plunge again into tragic crises: perfect plots for journalistic-television sagas. Generally, the impact on the financial markets of all this is low. For example, despite the ups and downs of Atalian politics, the spread has continued on its way, indifferent to everything but the ECB. Going on historical facts of weight, think that after the Japanese attack on Pearl Harbor in 1941 (which dragged the US into World War II) the stock index Dow Jones lost only 6% (and in the following 12 months it gained 2,20%).

Mass media

Newspapers, television. They bombard you with a continuous stream of news and data (often superficially explained), which lead you to deviate from your investment path (see point 2). Every day some economic data comes out: sometimes they improve, sometimes they get worse, but in the immediate future they rarely impact on your investments.

Just to say, during the last recession in the Eurozone (which began in March 2012 and ended in June 2013), Eurozone stock markets have gained about 13%. So, you focus on a few important things, check your wallet regularly, follow the right source of information, but do not be paranoid about the news.

Wanting to Become Successful Overnight

Do not be the investor who wants immediate success and who loses patience for daily highs and lows. One who wants quick results is certainly an example of how not to invest your savings if you want to succeed.

Successful investing is a bit like taking care of a vegetable garden. Plants grow slowly, the first few years give little fruits, but then start to grow faster. In general, it is foolish to expect significant results in a few weeks, months or even in a few years. Remember that you do not want to get rich fast, you want to get rich for sure.

Not Taking Profits

It may seem strange, but there are lots of investors that never take out their profits. This is detrimental since they never enjoy the money they earned through investing. It is like getting a gym subscription, but never going to the gym: it is useless and does not bring back to the practice.

The most successful investors always take out profits from time to time. Obviously, we are talking about calculated decisions and planned moves. However, the gold nugget here is the fact that if you do not have the money in your bank account, you cannot actually use it. It may sound silly, but it is a fact that most beginners tend to forget.

Chapter 4: How to Pick a Trading Service and a Broker

The use of shares, whether it is to collect dividends or to speculate on their listing, is an increasingly widespread and interesting practice. The risk of loss is always present but depending on the way you buy and sell your shares; this risk can be reduced. If you are wondering how to buy and sell the shares of large listed companies online, here are some explanations that may interest you.

Buy Shares to Become Shareholders

A large part of private individuals and institutions that buy Stocks do so to become shareholders.

It is the simplest use of actions and their main purpose.

In fact, when a company issues its shares, it is possible to buy them directly online.

However, for the already listed shares, to do so it is necessary to go through an intermediary, which can be an online broker or an online bank.

Of course, it is also possible to buy shares directly from sellers who have bought these shares previously, as well as you can re-sell your shares.

Buy and Sell Shares with Online Banks

The easiest way to buy and sell shares is to go through one of the placement products offered by banks and, in particular, by online banks. Thanks to 100% online operation of these banks, you can easily pass your purchase and sale orders directly via the internet without moving.

The advantages of this system are numerous because it is your bank that will take care of executing your orders and then buying and selling your shares. To take advantage of stock market shares through these systems, you must underwrite an Investment Plan in Shares, a securities account or life insurance, which are the main banking products on the stock market.

The only drawback of this method concerns the expenses that may be higher than those that you would have to pay if you bought and sold the shares yourself.

However, bank commissions rarely exceed 4%.

One of the main advantages of bank placement products is that your purchases and sales of shares are supervised by market intermediaries and you can benefit from advice.

Buy and Sell Shares with Online Brokers

Another method is to contact an online mediator. Their operation is almost identical to that of online banks, with the difference that you do not enjoy assistance and advice, but at the same time, the costs are lower because you decide for yourself what actions to buy or sell.

These online brokers also allow trading through stock market shares, without actually having to buy them. To do this, you just need to speculate on the evolution of their value. The tools that allow you to proceed in this way are CFDs.

Ultimately there are several methods to buy and sell shares on the internet. Before deciding on one or other of these solutions, take care to correctly evaluate the commissions involved as well as your level of knowledge on the stock exchange. Depending on these criteria, each of these two methods has different advantages. It is also good to understand the quotation system of an action to be able to speculate on this type of assets.

"How much does the purchase or sale of the shares cost?"

To answer this question, it is essential to define the strategy that will be adapted to buy or sell your shares.

If you own a stock portfolio through the intermediation of a stock market product, each investment in the purchase or sale will have a cost corresponding to the expenses called "brokerage expenses." These expenses can take various forms and involve different costs depending on the share traded (national, European or international market), the amount of the transaction carried out and, obviously, the intermediary. They can be in the form of a fixed or percentage cost on the amount of the transaction. It is therefore very important to carefully choose your stock market offer and your partner by consulting in advance the details of the charges applied to stock market orders.

Things are simpler for online trading and expenses are generally lower. In fact, to be sure, there are no defined brokerage fees for the sale or purchase of shares on the Stock Exchange from a trading platform through CFDs. Obviously, the mediator has a remuneration, however, but in a different and more transparent form: he applies the spread.

The spread corresponds to a small difference between the real quotation of an asset and the quotation of purchase or sale. As a result, when buying shares, the purchase price will be slightly higher than the real price of the asset in question and, in the case of a sale of shares, the selling price will be slightly lower than the real asset price.

Also, in this case, the spreads can vary from one broker to another and, depending on the type of shares you intend to sell or buy, it is interesting to compare the different spreads applied before opening your online account. The spreads can also be fixed and do not vary or be variable and evolve according to the market situation.

"What shares can be bought or sold online?"

For some years now, the offer of mediators in terms of CFDs on shares has been considerably enriched, and it is now possible to access many stocks from the trading platforms made available to the general public.

Of course, you will find European and international stocks. All the stocks proposed by these platforms are part of the large international stock indexes and are therefore particularly popular and volatile and offer many possibilities thanks to a precise strategy based on technical and fundamental data.

Chapter 5: Ways to Trade

The main method for investing in the forex market, therefore, remains the classic forex market. When you operate on the forex market, you are actually buying and selling currencies.

However, over the years, other financial instruments have been introduced to invest in forex and currencies indices on the forex exchange. We are talking about CFD (contract for difference) and binary options. The main feature of these two financial instruments is the following: when you use them to invest in forex, you will not actually own the lots you are investing in.

That said, for those who do not intend to trade online, it could make little sense. Let's try to clarify. Both CFDs and binary options are contracts between investors and brokers. It's not like the classic forex market, where traders buy and sell among themselves. In CFDs and binary options, the asset movement (in this case the buying and selling of currencies) does not take place.

CFDs and binary options are used to speculate on the performance of the value of equity securities. If the trader's forecast is correct, the operation will lead to a profit; vice versa, if the trader's prediction is wrong, the operation will lead to a loss. So, the mode of operation is similar to the stock market: if I invest on the upside, whether I do it with CFDs or actually buy currencies, I only earn money if the value increases.

As we explained in the previous paragraphs, CFDs are also derivative instruments, so they are used to speculate on the performance of asset values. This means that when you buy and sell CFDs, you will never own the asset traded (as opposed to classic forex trading).

Moreover, as with binary options, with CFDs it is possible to trade on:

- Equity securities

- Equity indices
- Forex currencies pairs
- Commodities
- ETF

Leverage plays an important role in CFD trading: through leverage, we can literally multiply the value of our investment. Just to give an example, if you use a lever of 1: 100 and invest € 100, thanks to this lever you can move well € 10,000 (using only your hundred!). All this is made possible thanks to the leverage, which is a sort of "loan" (if we can define it) by the broker, thanks to which you can invest more money than you really have.

But if we talk about eToro, we can't avoid talking about Social Trading. For those who do not know, eToro was the first broker to have introduced Social Trading in CFDs. Thanks to Social trading it is possible to invest by copying (automatically) the operations carried out by the other traders registered on the eToro platform. All you need is a couple of clicks to find the traders to follow, choose the amount to invest, and you're done. In this way, even novice traders can exploit the knowledge and experience of professional traders, copying their operations.

The online trading strategies are based on the study of mathematical and graphic analysis that can suggest the trader the best moment to buy and sell. As we have seen today, it is possible to invest in the stock market thanks to online trading, choosing between trading binary options and trading with the forex market.

Precise right away that there is no suitable trading strategy for all traders, but there are different trading strategies, based on traders and their style of trading. Therefore, it is possible to customize different online trading strategies on the basis of their trading objectives, their intellectual and psychological abilities.

We also recommend using 2 proven techniques not to turn winnings into losses:

stop loss: it establishes a maximum loss that you are willing to suffer;

take profit: you place a dynamic exit level that rises slowly.

Stocks vs. Other Investments

In this historical moment, the search for high returns has become almost spasmodic. Unfortunately, the expansionary policy of central banks has caused the collapse of yields (now virtually 0). Anyone who wants to get a positive return must take risks.

In this context, many are deciding to invest in stocks. What we are wondering with this chapter is whether it is really worth investing in stocks. The answer? It certainly is worth it, but it all depends on the modality of the investment.

This is an investment that can still guarantee very high performance, provided, however, to follow some guidelines.

The first tip is to use only really affordable platforms to invest in stocks. Among the best, we can definitely remember Plus500 or Markets. These platforms are characterized by the fact that they are very easy to use, even for those who have never worked with the actions but, at the same time, guarantee advanced tools, suitable even for the most experienced and needs. At the time of registration, you receive a free bonus that amounts to 7,000 euros for Plus500 and 4,000 euros for Markets. This is additional capital that can be used to operate on the stock markets but cannot be directly withdrawn. If you use the bonus and you get profits, these profits can instead be taken without problems and without constraints.

Both Plus500 and Markets are Trading Contracts for Difference (CFD) trading platforms: this is a particularly flexible and easy-to-understand derivative instrument that guarantees the possibility of obtaining high profits both when markets rise and fall. This is the second condition that makes it worthwhile to invest in stocks: if you buy shares directly, you earn only when the markets go up. And in today's financial conditions, it's an immense gamble. At this time, it is absolutely not convenient to buy shares, the thing that must be done is to subscribe to derivatives (such as CFDs that are very simple) that have underlying actions. Plus500 and Markets are the ideal solutions for investing in stocks and, incidentally, they also allow investing in forex, indices, commodities, bitcoins, etc.

If you want to invest in shares and you want to earn money, the advice is to open an account on Markets or on Plus500.

Leverage — The Huge Advantage of Stock Investing

Through the use of financial leverage (or simply "leverage"), a person has the possibility to buy or sell financial assets for an amount higher than the capital held and, consequently, to benefit from a higher potential return than that deriving from a direct investment in the underlying and, conversely, to expose yourself to the risk of very significant losses.

Let's see how the concept of leverage works starting from a simple case. Let's assume you have $ 100 available to invest Leverage financial in a stock. Let's assume that the gain or loss expectations are equal to 30%: if things go well, we will have $ 130; otherwise, we will have $ 70. This is simple speculation in which we bet on a particular event.

In case we decide to risk more investing, in addition to our $ 100, also another $ 900 borrowed, then the investment would take a different articulation because we use the leverage of 10 to 1 (we invest $ 1000 having a capital initial only of 100). If things go well and the stock goes up 30%, we will receive $ 1300, we return the 900 borrowed with a gain of $ 300 on initial capital of 100. So, we get a 300% profit with a stock that in he gave a 30% return. Obviously, on the $ 900 borrowed, we will have to pay interest, but the general principle remains valid: the leverage allows to increase the possible gains.

Considering the further case of the investment in derivatives. Let's assume we buy a derivative that, within a month, gives the right to buy 100 grams of gold at a price set today of $ 5,000. We could physically buy the gold with an outlay of 5000 $ and keep it waiting for the price to rise and then sell it back. If we decide instead to use derivatives, we should not have $ 5,000, but only the capital needed to buy the derivative. Let's say that a bank sells for 100 $ the derivative that allows us to buy the same 100 grams of gold in a month to $ 5,000. If in a month the gold is worth 5,500, we can buy it and sell it immediately, realizing a gain of 500 $. With the 100 $ of the price of the derivative, we make a profit of $ 400, or 400%, at $ 100.

Without using derivatives and leverage, with the same $500, I could have earned them only against an investment of $5,000, making a profit of 10%.

What are the potentials of its use?

The potential of leveraging is clear. But be careful: the leverage multiplier effect, described with the previous examples, works even if the investment goes wrong. For example, if we decide to invest $ 100 in our possession plus an additional sum of $ 900 borrowed, if the stock depreciated by 30%, we would remain with only $ 700 in hand; having to return the $ 900 borrowed plus interest and considering the $ 100 of our initial investment we would have a loss of over $ 300 on an initial capital of $ 100. As a percentage, the loss would, therefore, be 300% against a reduction in the value of the share of 30%.

Another element to keep in mind is that the different financial levers can be combined: in this way speculation operations are carried out using a "squared lever" with clear reflections on potential potentials.

What may appear to be an interesting tool with positive potential for the investor, on the other hand, presents risks that must, therefore, be taken into due consideration. In fact, if the financial system, as a whole, works with very high leverage and financial institutions lend money to each other to multiply the possible profits, the loss of an individual investor can trigger a domino effect by infecting the entire financial market.

Banks are typically entities that operate with a more or less high degree of leverage: against a certain net capital, the total assets in which the resources are invested is generally much higher. For example, a bank with equity of $ 100 and leverage of 20 manages assets for $ 2,000. A loss of 1% of the assets entails the loss of 20% of the equity capital.

The development of the market for the transfer of credit risk (from financial intermediaries to the market) has meant that the traditional bank model, called "originate-and-hold" ("create and hold:" the bank that provided the loan it remains in the balance sheet until maturity), has been substituted for many operators from the "originate-to-distribute" ("create and distribute:" the intermediary selects the debtors, but then transfers the loan to others, recovering the liquidity and the regulatory capital previously committed or the pure credit risk (credit derivatives), with benefits only on capital requirements), with the effect of a further increase in leverage. The spread of this second bank model is one of the factors that explain the crisis triggered on the sub-prime mortgage market.

Property price inflation has supported the issuance of securitized loans and the exponential growth of the related market, allowing banks to make huge profits and, at the same time, increase leverage. But "the money machine" could not last long and in the end, many banks found themselves without sufficient capital to absorb the losses deriving from the inversion of the real estate market trend, resulting in fact as failed companies.

In the meantime, the example of the banks has spread within the financial system by spreading to all other financial institutions: leverage had prevailed, especially in the United States, generating a huge volume of risky investments that rested on a fraction infinitesimal of equity capital. We are thinking of the issue of so-called "credit default swaps" (derivative instruments used to hedge against the default risk of the debtor). Some insurance companies were heavily exposed to the real estate market, and when the latter collapsed and the value of mortgages fell, they began to lose without having sufficient capital to absorb the losses deriving from the issue of those instruments.

In order not to risk failing and return to sufficient levels of bank capital, capital increases can be used (not an easy task in times of crisis), the reduction of the amount of loans to businesses (granting fewer new loans and not renewal of those already issued) and the disposal of other liquid assets (mostly shares). The result of all this, in the period of the sub-prime crisis, was a credit freeze and a collapse of the stock market. These are the main channels through which the financial crisis has hit the real economy. Credit rationing affected investments and the fall in the stock market (which adds to the decline in house prices) has reduced the value of household wealth and therefore consumption.

We know that a certain level of leverage is physiological to sustain economic growth, even if we have no indication of what the optimal level is. But history teaches us how in an increasingly globalized and interdependent economic-financial system, leverage can be a trigger for speculative bubbles. And it is in these periods that the strongest disconnection between finance and the real economy is generated.

Earning Potential

The stock market gives the false impression that making money on the stock market is just a matter of choosing the right securities, investing quickly, staying glued to a computer screen and spending the day obsessing over what the investment is. But the truth about how to make money on the stock market is another, and you'll find out by reading the following pages.

The secret that reveals how to earn on the Stock Exchange, buying or selling securities and shares, is well explained by the thought of an investor known throughout the world, Benjamin Graham:
"Real money is made not by buying and selling, but by owning the securities, receiving interest and dividends and taking advantage of the increase in their value in the long term."

More simply, the first secret to understanding how to earn on the stock market according to Graham is to focus on long-term investments, keeping a stock for at least 5 years in your investment portfolio.

Including the first fundamental concept of investing in the stock market, we now concretely analyze how to earn by buying stocks.

Investing in the stock market, buying and selling stocks, for many people is a very attractive prospect. However, we are talking about a real investment, accompanied by risk, and it is necessary to understand that it is not easy to earn on the stock market as some want to make believe.

To understand how to do this, we need to be aware of what we are doing and what are the factors that influence the success or failure of our investment.

Many prefer to turn to a financial advisor and leave it to him to follow the market trend, while others more enterprising opt for the choice to invest through CFD or to buy shares through an intermediary.

On the stock exchange, you earn and lose, and the certainty of the result is not always quantifiable. That's why it is essential to know what the mechanisms of gain and loss are on the stock market and, therefore, how to earn on the stock market, as well as knowing how the stock market works.

Investing in the stock market, buying or selling shares, involves investing in one or more of the many companies listed on the stock exchange, both in America and abroad. Companies have an interest in listing on the Stock Exchange to find new financial resources necessary for their production processes. The investor does not invest for the glory or to favor one company over another, but to have a profit and to earn the difference between the purchase price and the selling price.

But how to make money with stock market shares? Every little saver can decide to invest part of his savings in shares, that is fractions of corporate capital traded on the stock exchange.

Assume that today in some shares have a nominal value of 11.00 euros and a market value of 12.50 euros thanks to an appreciation of the stock following a statement by the company's ad on a contract in North Europe.

The investor wants to earn on the stock exchange and decides to buy 10,000 of those shares through an intermediary. The cost of investing in the stock market will be the number of shares for the price per share. In our case, it is 125.000 euro (12.50 * 10.000), to which must be added commission costs for the operation, which vary from intermediary to intermediary.

The following week, the same shares recorded a rise following the positive result of the quarterly report. The price of those share rises to 13.80, a price higher than that to which the investor has paid the shares (12.50).

The investor decides to sell the 10,000 shares bought the previous week. The broker will give the investor the current value of the shares. This will then have to return 138,000 euros (13.80 * 10,000), then withholding the amount of the commission.

And here is explained how to earn on the stock market.

The realized gain is obtained with the difference between the sale value (or € 138,000 - commissions) and the purchase cost of the securities (i.e., € 125,000 + commissions): in our example, we have a profit of € 12,750.00 (137,850- 125,100).

But if the price of the shares fell, however, from 12.50 to 10.00 euros and the investor had decided to sell, then the result would be a loss.

Penny Stocks

There are two things that trading penny stocks are very much known for:

- You can quickly make a big amount of money.
- There is a high probability that you will lose your investment.

These are two opposing extremes that you will be facing. Of course, your objective is to rake in serious profits. Unfortunately, the majority of people who trade penny stocks fail to make any positive return. In fact, they lose their money. But do not be discouraged; because there are still people out there, the well-experienced and real expert traders who double, triple, and continuously grow their money more than you can ever imagine.

Losing trade is normal. Even well-experienced traders make the wrong investment decisions from time to time. However, you must avoid such mistakes as much as possible. Now, to help cut down your future losses, you should be aware of the risks that you will be facing when you trade penny stocks.

The Risks

Small Companies

The majority of the companies in the penny stock market are small companies. In fact, they can be so small that they do not even meet the minimum capitalization requirement. You will find many of these companies on the Pink Sheets. But then again, as discussed in the previous book, do not buy penny stocks from the Pink Sheets. Since they are small companies, it is hard to tell if they are stable enough and if they will even grow. Many small companies also tend to be less professional. Sometimes the executives of a small company see and treat the assets of the company, including the stocks and penny shares, as their own personal belonging.

Start-Up Companies

Many of the companies that issue penny stocks are start-up companies. Therefore, they tend to have a very limited history that you can track. This makes it risky because you would not know for sure if the business is legitimate or if the company is operating a scam.

Less Transparent

Penny stocks do not have stringent requirements. You can always buy them on the Pink Sheets or over the counter (OTC). Remember that the companies on the Pink Sheets are not required to file with the SEC and to meet the minimum capitalization requirements or capital stock of a legitimate company.

Many companies on the Pink Sheets only reveal very limited information about their business, so it is hard to get sufficient and accurate data. Worse, some companies operate a scam.

Bankruptcy

The penny stock market is not only participated by small and start-up companies, but it also has companies that are about to go bankrupt. Unfortunately, these struggling companies will not reveal that they are already about to declare bankruptcy and will even make their stocks to look like an attractive investment. Of course, there is still a probability of making a good amount of profit when you invest in a company that is struggling to survive, especially when the company is able to save itself from bankruptcy and begin to grow successfully. However, the probability of such an ideal scenario to happen is small. Trading penny stocks are already risky enough; you would not want to take more risks.

The reason why you should not invest in a company that is about to go bankrupt is that you will run the risk of losing everything. Once the company declares bankruptcy and does not have sufficient assets to cover all its debts and obligations to its creditors, you will not be able to get your money back.

Low Liquidity

Penny stocks have low liquidity. With low liquidity, they become open to manipulation. A common type of fraudulent scheme is the pump and dump, in which the value of certain penny stocks are pumped up using some fraudulent marketing hype to convince traders to buy them. As its name already implies, the price of certain stocks is pumped up using some promotional or marketing hype. In turn, traders will find the stocks attractive and make an investment. The penny stocks are then dumped on the traders, and their value begins to fall down.

Take note that the pump and dump scheme can be applied even if the company is actually doing well. In fact, when the company is making profits, the pump and dump scheme will be harder to detect. By adding a few dollars on the price of certain stocks that are already increasing, it is almost impossible for traders to determine whether the increased total value is due to legitimate means or merely a result of a pump and dump scheme.

Speculative

Due to so many factors that affect the prices of penny stocks, it can be said that the penny stock market is highly speculative. An important thing in trading penny stocks is first to buy the stocks that truly have a good value. Unfortunately, with the increasing number of scams, hackers, and frauds out there, it becomes difficult to know whether you are really purchasing a good stock or merely a stock whose value is being pumped. Second, even if you get to buy a profitable stock, many active factors can affect its performance in the market. The best stock today may no longer be considered a good stock by tomorrow, depending on the circumstances. Also, granting that the prices of your penny stocks increase, will the buyers still see them attractive and profitable by the time you want to sell them?

These, among many other things, are the risks faced by traders of penny stocks. Consider also the sad fact that most traders fail to make any profit and simply lose their investment.

Do you think you are up for the challenge? If your entrepreneurial spirit is not crushed by these risks, then get ready for the awesome benefits of trading penny stocks.

The Benefits

Trading penny stocks are one of the best investment opportunities that offer wonderful benefits. So, if you honestly think that you can manage the abovementioned risks, then welcome to the world of high profits — a place where you can double, triple, or even multiply your money by more than 20 times in a short period.

Price

Penny stocks are cheap. A single penny stock only costs less than $5. If you have a lot of money to invest, then you can have thousands of stocks from different companies. If you are on a shoestring budget, then this opportunity is also available to you.

High Potential Return

When you trade penny stocks, there is a potential to multiply the value of your stocks many times over. In fact, there is a potential for the prices of your stocks to double within 24 hours or less.

Unlike blue-chip stocks where a 60% increase is considered a big profit already, such is considered normal when you trade penny stocks. And, unlike binary options where you can gain 90% but has a much higher risk, trading penny stocks can make your money grow by more than 500% within a short period. Also, since the penny stock market is mostly composed of small businesses, there is a high probability for the value of their penny stocks to grow, since small businesses have a lot of space for improvements.

High Volume

You can have thousands of penny stocks for a small amount. Having a high volume of penny stocks is good, especially if you get them from a start-up company that is doing well.

Low or Controlled Risk

Penny stocks are inexpensive. You do not have to purchase a lot of penny stocks to earn a decent amount of profit. You can also diversify your stocks to help minimize your losses. And, unlike trading binary options where you will lose your whole wager when you make a wrong investment decision, you can still keep your penny stocks and sell them. If you are patient enough, there is really no such thing as a permanent loss. Considering the volatility of penny stocks, even if the value of your penny stocks decreases, there is a good chance that it will increase after some time.

Chapter 6: When to Buy and Sell

Since this is a guide for beginners and most people that start out decide to begin their investing journey with stocks, we thought it would be interesting to lay out the foundation of the topic. For those who choose to invest in stocks, the objective is undoubtedly that of obtaining the highest possible remuneration from their investment, which is why the choice of securities on which to invest their money is of fundamental importance.

Invest in Stocks

In this regard, there are no universally valid and reliable rules that allow you to obtain good earnings and eliminate risks of losses; otherwise, the number of investors would be much higher.

In other words, the safe stocks to invest in, if they had ever existed in the past, today are officially extinct! However, this does not mean that plans cannot be made to reduce risk while maintaining a high level of profit. Those who choose to invest in shares today are perfectly aware that there are some parameters that experts believe are essential to consider when identifying the shares to be included in an investment portfolio. These parameters are the capitalization of the company, the profitability of equity, the ratio between profit and price, the ratio of Ratio to price book value, the dividend yield and the ratings/target price. Let's see what these individual parameters consist of in detail, and how we can use them to choose the stocks to invest in today.

Capitalization of Companies

Although this is a very often underestimated parameter, we must nevertheless consider that the size of the company is very often a sign of market power, in most cases through the possession of brands or technologies exploited globally. The use of this parameter, however, makes sense especially for equity investments in the US market, where over the last year companies with high capitalization (Apple, Coca Cola, Facebook, Google, Amazon, etc.) have seen a significant performance. The close relationship existing in the US shareholding between the level of capitalization on the stock exchange and the performance of the stock is one of the factors underlying the growing weight that American stocks have in the portfolios of international investors. The interest of traders in US stocks has also increased in light of the boom in listed companies operating in the tech and web segment.

Return over Equity (RoE)

This is the ratio between the net result and the net assets of a given company. In particular, from the point of view of equity investments is an important parameter as profitability higher than the cost of capital is an index of the ability of an enterprise to create value. From this point of view, the Roe is always held in strong consideration by those who choose to invest in shares today.

Price/Earnings Ratio

A low ratio of this parameter makes a share price particularly attractive, but at the same time, it could mean that expectations regarding future profits are not particularly positive. As in the case of the Roe, this is a factor to be taken into consideration when choosing the best stocks to invest in.

Price/Value Ratio

The ratio between the share price and the net asset value resulting from the last balance sheet, especially if this ratio is lower than the unit means that the company is being paid less than the value of the budget net of liabilities. However, this does not necessarily mean that it is a good deal, since the company may not be able to produce profits either.

Dividend Yield

This is the percentage ratio between the last distributed dividend and the share price. In particular, it measures the remuneration provided by the company to shareholders in the last year in the form of liquidity. This parameter is often taken into account to identify the stocks to invest in since a company is able to distribute dividends is generally a healthy company. But also, in this case, as with all the other selection parameters, it is necessary to make a broader and more complete analysis since a high level of this indicator could also mean that the company has made few investments or has little prospect of growth. For this reason, looking at the dividend yield as a primary factor in determining the securities on which to invest in the stock market is reductive. The dividend yield only makes sense if accompanied by considerations on any business plans and industrial plans of the listed company. Only in this way is it possible to have guarantees on what are the prospects of the group in the future.

Rating and Target Price

The rating is the judgment that certain analysts and investment banks have on specifically listed security while the target price represents the maximum target price to which the shares may reach. Dozens of judgments are published daily on all listed shares. Giving an eye to these judgments is a way to have further clarification on what may be the prospects of the listed. If, in fact, more brokers decide to cut the rating on an X stock from buy to neutral or worse sell, then it means that, indeed, the expectations of the security in question are certainly not positive and therefore, perhaps, it is not the case to insert this title in the list of shares to invest in.

Clearly, promotions and failures (upgrades and downgrades) are not in the air but are accompanied by reports within which are explained the reasons behind that single judgment. Therefore, rating and target price are one of the most important factors for choosing the best stocks to invest in. As the great traders who focus on equities perfectly know, by looking at the history or the evolution of the rating and target price of a single stock, one can have an even more complete picture in the choice of actions to invest in today.

These are the main indicators that will dictate whether your investment will be successful or not. Taking time to study the structure of the company you want to invest in is extremely important since it gives you the opportunity to get a better idea of where it is going and what it is aiming at for the future. Remember that when you invest in stocks, you own part of that project: it is your duty to understand it fully.

Here are some terms that you should familiarize with if you want to get better at stock investing.

One who wants to invest or play on the stock exchange cannot consider or know some terms which are basic for their trading actions. Some precautions must be taken into consideration:

- read constantly and daily, newspapers of an economic nature; this will mainly serve those who are not very familiar with the terminology used and consequently do not know the meaning of Actions, Bots, BTPs, Dow Jones, Nasdaq, Nikkei, etc.
- Watch economic news regularly, in such a way as to familiarize yourself and learn how to pronounce the most used terms;
- Document yourself through books, forums, and online sites. This will greatly facilitate understanding and will also serve as personal cultural baggage. In this way, you can increase your knowledge and take your first steps in the world of economics.

A first term to know is certainly the word *share*, which is the cardinal element of the companies, which represents in all respects a share of the social capital of a company. The shares can be divided mainly into 3 categories:

1. **Ordinary Shares**: according to which the holder can express his right to vote;
2. **Savings Shares**: there is no possibility to cast a vote but give a greater dividend than previous shares;
3. **Preference Shares**: guarantee "a greater privilege" in the allocation of profits and voting power in extraordinary shareholders' meetings.

Chapter 7: Long-Term Investing vs. Day Trading

Very often the concepts of saving and investing are confused, as well as that of "saver" and "trader." However, there are substantial differences that need to be understood, before diving deeper into the subject of money.

In this second chapter, we will explain what saving and investing are, analyzing which choice is more convenient today.

Saving means taking out a portion of income received, that you deliberately choose not to consume immediately, but to store in a bank account for the future. Saving often results in the tranquillity guaranteed by the availability of resources to deal with unexpected situations.

Savings can then be allocated to investment, and this is the main analogy between the two concepts. The investment may be of the "economic" type (such as the purchase of a car or company machinery), or of the "financial" type (such as the purchase of a security or mutual fund with the objective to see capital growth over time). However, unlike savings, in the case of investing, the achievement of the desired objective is not certain (for example, a stock may lose value) so the result can be negative, compromising the amounts saved.

"Which is better?"

If the question that arises is whether it is better to save or invest, the answer is probably "both." The choice depends on your financial situation and your personal goals.

Savings can be used to invest, but it can also be used in other ways. In fact, the money saved can also be deposited in the bank to reduce risks (theft). But this, unlike what many thinks, is a wrong and unprofitable choice: money, in fact, tends to lose purchasing power over time due to inflation. In other words, if you save 100 Dollars today, in 20 years, you will be able to get less out of that money than today. This is why saving money is, often, the wrong choice if you want to get wealthy.

Assuming an average increase in the cost of living around 2% and a saved sum of 5,000 Dollars, in five years this sum will fall to real 4,500 Dollars, that is 10% less (excluding banking taxes!). Obviously, you can keep the savings at home (under the classic mattress!), But with all the risks that come with it.

"What is the difference between trading and saving?"

Let's repeat it once again to get it better. Saving means to put money aside little by little to accumulate a certain sum. Usually, you save for a certain goal, like going on vacation, buying a car or for emergencies that could happen.

Instead, trading means taking a part of the money to make it grow, buying tools that can increase its value like currencies, real estates and ETF's.

"Who should save?"

Obviously, everyone should try to save a part of their money. The rule is to have away on your bank account at least the necessary to "survive" for three months and cover the main expenses (such as food and rent). This will offer air pocket, in case of inconvenient and unexpected situations.

Saving is, therefore, a rule and as every good rule has its exceptions. You can, in fact, stop putting aside the money when:

- you have too much debt, and you are trying to pay it off;
- the family has priority and could not go on in case of unfortunate events to one of its members.

Even when you have set aside enough for emergencies, you do not have to stop saving. The goal of everyone should be to put aside at least 10% of their salary every month, perhaps starting from 5% and gradually scaling up. To make things easier, you can save money by thinking of any objective; like having enough money for a great honeymoon or to get a new car.

Having a goal is essential, so you know what you're saving for. Every reach person has financial goals, so it is a good habit to pick up.

"When is the time to trade?"

Like when you save money, you need to have a goal to when and how to trade your savings. In this case, it is important to know what your short, medium and long-term goals are.

- With "short term" we mean goals for the next 3 years;
- With "medium term," things are planned for the next 3-10 years
- The "long-term" goals are those for which you will not need the money back for at least 10 years or more

For short-term objectives, you usually invest through deposit accounts, which allow you to get a minimum return in a short amount of time. However, this has been a bit shrinking in the last period (deposit rates are at the lowest). For the medium-long term objectives, it is instead advisable to invest in the market, to avoid the reduction in value that inflation produces on "still" money. The market usually guarantees higher returns than deposit accounts over longer periods and having a well-constructed portfolio helps a lot in this regard.

For those approaching or exceeding 30 years of age, having a medium-long term goal is advisable. Investing and setting aside money for retirement can be a good start.

To sum up the concept, everything depends on your time horizon:

1. If you think about using the money within one or three years, save it.
2. If you do not need this money for the next 10 years, invest it.

If, on the other hand, you plan on using the savings in the next 5 or 10 years, but you want to still have money set aside in your bank account, then you will have to do both. Keep in mind that this is much harder and requires more discipline. However, with the right mindset, it is certainly the best option.

"What does trading wisely mean?"

Since the importance of the investment is well established, it should also be emphasized that there is no recipe to guarantee the success of an investment.

However, following some prudential rules can help minimize risks.

First of all, we need to avoid the dream of making money overnight. On the market, there are professional operators, experts, who dedicate all their time to this activity, but they often make mistakes as well. Just to say how difficult it is and how "get rich quick schemes" do not exist.

One strategy that every investor needs to master to reduce the risk is diversification. This means not putting all your eggs in one basket but, rather, spreading your resources on different assets. When the invested amount grows it becomes more important to diversify not only between the asset classes (stocks, bonds, commodities) but also geographically (considering the currency variable) and size-wise (small or big cap companies to stay within the equity, more or less long maturities for government securities, bonds with different level of risk in the corporate sphere).

Making these choices takes time, that needs to be subtracted from work or other activities. So, in the end, it is about investing time, before moving the money. But it is worth it and, frankly speaking, the only option to avoid reckless choices that you may regret afterward.

Chapter 8: Predicting the Market

Indicators and charts are one of the most important components when we talk about technical analysis. In addition to experience, coldness, and psychology, a good analyst cannot disregard a thorough knowledge of the graphs. The latter can represent different information and may appear in different forms.

In graphical analysis, the graphs deserve particular attention because they represent the price dynamics of a given financial instrument and in a given period.

In the technical analysis, the most commonly used type of graph is certainly the candlestick chart, better known under the name of a Japanese candlestick chart. Before moving on to a detailed description of the candlestick chart, however, I would like to say a few words about two other charts, less used than candlestick charts, but which may be useful as they can help you understand the Japanese candlestick chart.

The price chart is shown on a Cartesian plane where, on the abscissa axis, that is the vertical axis the time is reported, while on the horizontal axis the price is reported.

Given this premise, we can still say that the graphs refer to different time periods whether they are fractions of minutes, hours and days, if not even weeks, months or even years indicating different sizes of opening or closing, of maximums and minima.

On the axis of the abscissas, we find a space called histogram of the volume, which represents the number of instruments exchanged during the period under examination.

In graphic analysis, in the specific and more generally in the technical analysis, various types of graph are used.

Features of a Good Chart

With the above, I do not mean that you will need a chart that contains a myriad of information or detailed information in detail, but I would like to emphasize that the best successful traders on the market, use very few indicators. Yes, you understood correctly. only a few indicators. You will, therefore, think that what has been described up to now is only a chat, but it is not so, as these extrapolate the most important information directly from the graph. The charts obviously can only be provided by the brokers, which as for the forex market, here too we advise you always to choose the best binary options brokers. So, it is not true that the graphics are all the same, it will be a good broker who will extrapolate all the information that interests him from the various detailed charts. And from here, we recognize the best brokers.

The reason for this extrapolation is very simple: since the indicators express only the past in a graphic form, they can provide a very approximate vision of the future. So too many indicators in a chart can sometimes create confusion instead of aid.

Therefore, we consider it very important to keep the following points in mind:

- **Good graphics program** - With this, in fact, you should always be able to look far enough in the past, to plan the future and identify relevant barriers and gather a satisfactory overview. In the binary options charts of the different brokers, this time frame is too narrow to draw reliable conclusions.
- **Good quality graphs always indicate different time intervals.** These range from a few minutes to a max. of a month.
- **Never set just a common linear chart.** This fact would not be very useful for technical analysis purposes. On the other hand, candle or beam charts are used, which we will explain briefly.

"What is chart analysis?"

The analysis of the graphs is above all the search for particular shapes, also called graphic structures, configurations, figures.

They are figures that emerge from the price movement, and that can signal its future trend. They are tracked by analysts joining points in the price graph of financial security or the performance of an indicator.

The purpose of the graphic analysis will, therefore, be to identify the most typical price patterns for forecasting purposes.

These graphic formations can be classified into different categories. The main categories of classes can assume inversion or continuation or consolidation characteristics. The fundamental feature will also be the dynamics of the volumes, which we will explain under each figure.

This is why it takes technique, experience, strategies, if not the analyst's ability to see these forms in the movement of a graph. These are the fundamental elements of this type of analysis. The concept of the trendline, support, and resistance are also part of this aspect of technical analysis.

Most Used Graphs for Graphic Analysis

Below we will list the most used graphs for graphic analysis and explain the operation. Before doing this, however, we must explain another very important and used concept: the figure of Continuation. These have common characteristics in all the graphs, they represent a pause in the prevailing trend in progress and are a prelude to a continuation of the trend in the direction of the direction previously underway. For this reason, they are also known as consolidation figures.

The main difference between the continuation and the inversion figures concerns the extension.

The continuation figures are often accompanied by a decrease in the volumes traded.

One of the first figures we are going to examine is the wedge.

Wedge

This too is a continuation figure on explained and is very similar to the triangle for 2 reasons:

- for the form;
- for the time it takes to form. This differs from the triangle that we will see below because the shape that forms is characterized by a strongly bullish or bearish inclination opposite to that of the current trend.

This means that:

- this chart consists of two convergent trendlines and takes about one to three months to develop;
- in an uptrend, a falling wedge or "a descending wedge" can be encountered; while in a bearish tendency, a rising wedge or "an ascending wedge" can develop.

As with the pennant and flag figures, the wedge can be found in the middle of a movement, thus allowing to calculate minimum targets.

The dynamics of the volumes see a decrease in the course of the formation of the pattern, and it should go to be reduced for all the period of formation of the figure. On the contrary, they increase significantly when the trendline is broken, which is a typical feature of the wedge.

The second figure we examine in this chapter is the pennant.

Pennant

This figure is also quite common in chart analysis.

This figure together with the figure of the flag, which we will see immediately after the flag appears after an almost vertical movement and represents a pause in the trend.

Its characteristic is that it is presented as a symmetrical triangle which, however, has a maximum extension of 3 weeks. Most often, in bearish actions, the refinement time of the figure is even lower and is equal to one or maximum two weeks. The pennant is halfway to the bullish or bearish movement, with the obvious implications in calculating the minimum targets for the movement's arrival.

It will, therefore, be obvious that the volume decreases during the formation of the figure and should be low throughout the formation of the pattern. On the contrary, instead, they significantly increase when the trendline breaks, which identifies the pennant. These are accompanied by a similar trend in the range within which prices move.

Pennants most often coincide with a contraction phase, which does not necessarily have an opposite inclination with respect to the basic trend.

Both this figure and the next develop within a rather short time frame.

The third figure that we examine as announced is the Flag.

Flag

Flag formation, or flag, is a very common pattern of continuation in the graphic analysis. This form tends to appear close to the temporary exhaustion of a trend, which represents a brief pause in the market after strongly accentuated movements, are almost vertical and known as the flagpole.

The flag has a shape similar to a parallelepiped, almost to represent a rectangle, bounded by two parallel trendlines but opposed to the prevailing trend; in other words, it can be seen as a flag that is tilted downward in an uptrend and upward in a bearish trend.

His training ends within a medium period, that is between one and three weeks. It usually appears halfway to complete the movement.

It must also be said that if it is in a bearish movement the perfection time is less and the figure is usually completed in one or two weeks. Precisely because it is in the middle of the bullish or bearish movement, the figure is important for identifying price targets. From here we will then calculate the width of the movement preceding the flag and report this distance after the break of the trendline delineating the figure.

The volume should also decrease during the formation of the figure and then increase again when the trendline is broken.

So, let's see how to use Flag and Pennant.

The targets that can be identified in relation to these figures are two:

- The first is determined by projecting the width of the base from the breakout point; here this target assumes less importance if we consider the reduced dimensions of the figure.
- The second can instead be obtained by projecting, from the breakout point, a distance equivalent to that covered by the movement that preceded the formation of the pennant.
- This means that these figures often materialize around half of the overall movement, giving a fair advantage at the operational level.

The temporary phase of price weakness can be exploited to enter the stock or even just to increase the position taken earlier, again using a stop-loss much lower than the potential take-profit.

The fourth figure that we will explain will be represented by the rectangle.

Rectangle

The rectangle is the simplest among the figures proposed by the technical analysis.

It identifies a phase of price congestion. In Technical Analysis, with this term, we mean a graphic formation in correspondence with which prices oscillate within a narrow range of values. This process takes place when the market moves sideways.

The pattern represents a break zone of the current trend in which prices move sideways. This also gives rise to the name of the trading range or congestion area, a figure that represents a period of consolidation of the current trend that is resolved in the direction of the trend that preceded it. This represents a fundamental figure, to correctly identify the continuation pattern if not also the observation of the volumes.

Also, for this bullish figure, the rebounds must be accompanied by high volumes, with the corrections characterized by decreasing volumes. In the opposite case, instead, in the bearish rectangle, are the corrections to have more accentuated volumes.

Many investors, take advantage of the oscillations, selling to the top of the figure and buying at the minimum. However, those who use this approach risk not exploiting the breaking of the pattern.

The figure in question usually takes from one to three months to improve, and the minimum target is represented by the translation of the height of the rectangle when the price breaks the figure.

Prices move within a fixed band identified by support and resistance as better shown in the figure below.

first target 1

The rectangles can also be configured as inversion figures, depending on the context in which they are formed. It is therefore evident how the congestion phases identify a moment in which the market expresses considerable uncertainty and awaits new information to decide the future trend. Unlike the contraction phases (in which the continuous reduction in volatility identifies in an increasingly precise manner the moment in which the market will receive the information that awaits) a figure of congestion like the rectangle does not allow to identify sufficiently in advance the moment in which the breakout will take place.

The operational cues that this figure can provide are basically of two types:

1. The first requires waiting for the exit of prices from the congestion zone initially identified. This exit must necessarily be classified as a breakout and therefore must be characterized by an increase in volumes and volatility.
2. The second operational step derives from the possibility of exploiting the lateral movement of prices to buy close to the identified support and sell when the values are near the top of the figure again.

Support and Resistance

Let me now explain briefly what the supports and the resistances are.

Support is defined as that price level at which there is, an arrest of the downward trend in prices. An excessive concentration of purchases that occurs in the vicinity of the same will cause a block in the downward trend in prices.

A level of support is defined as reliable when it shows resistance to repeated "attacks" without a bearish breakdown.

The Resistance is defined instead as that level of price where the growth of the same stops. In the case of the Resistance, the high concentration of sales prevents the continuation of the increase. A resistance level, on the contrary, is stronger and more reliable as it resists repeated "attacks" without an upward failure. Surely, a historical minimum or maximum represents a level of Support or Strategic Resistance.

Consequently, the penetration or breaking of support levels or even resistance can be caused by:

- important changes in the fundamental values of a company (increase in profits, changes in management, etc.);
- from simple forecasts based on price trends in recent times;
- both levels of support and resistance can also arise from motivations exclusively of an emotional nature. Supports and resistances represent with great simplicity the encounter/clash between supply and demand.

From the above it is clear that in practice, a breakout, or an event in which the price comes out of a trend, breaking a support or resistance or a channel, above a level of resistance evidence an increase in demand, arising from more buyers, who are willing to buy at higher prices than the current ones.

In the opposite case, instead, the breakdown of support shows an increase in the sellers, and therefore in the offer, as more sellers are willing to sell even at lower prices than the current ones.

If a level of support is broken, it automatically turns into a resistance level, just as if a resistance level is broken, it becomes a level of support. This process is known as a pullback, which is a time when a trending market takes a break.

The support and resistance lines can be drawn horizontally and then we will talk about static support, where the support corresponds to a precise and constant point in time; both obliquely and in this case, we will talk about dynamic support, where a trendline is drawn with the variation of prices and with the passage of time.

The fifth figure concerns the triangle.

Triangle

In technical analysis, that of the triangle is a consolidation figure and is used to verify the continuation of the main trend. This is a pattern that lasts a few months when there is a pause in the current trend with prices that oscillate in an increasingly narrow area.

The figure has the following characteristics:

- The triangle must have a minimum of four reaction points; two superiors, and two inferiors; the first ones necessary to trace the upper trendline, the seconds necessary to draw the lower trend line.
- The triangle is characterized by a time limit for its resolution. Usually, the prices break the triangle at a point between two thirds and three-quarters of the depth of the triangle.
- The volumes in the formation phase of the triangle waves lose strength and then explode when the trendline that delimits the figure breaks.
- The minimum target for price trends is calculated by projecting the maximum height of the triangle.

The figure in question can present itself according to three different structures:

Symmetrical Triangle

The Symmetrical Triangle has the trendlines that delimit it that are convergent.

Prices tend to move in a range that gradually becomes narrower with the passing of the sessions, due to a constant reduction of the maximums, and also due to a constant reduction of the minimums.

Descending Triangle (characterized by a flat demarcation line, the lower one, and by a bearish trend line, the upper one.)

In this figure, there will be a greater conviction on the part of the bearish and is often found during a downward trend.

The reduction in the range within which prices move, occurs only thanks to an increase in the minimum, while the maximums remain almost unchanged.

Just such behavior makes evident the greater pressure of the buyers with respect to the sellers and attributes to this figure a bullish value.

Descending triangle

The figure represents a symmetrical structure, which makes it difficult to interpret. In the third case, on the other hand, we speak of an ascending triangle, characterized by an upper line of flat demarcation and a line, the lower, ascending line. This pattern indicates a greater strength of the uptrend and is often found during an uptrend

Regardless of the configuration, whether symmetrical, ascending or descending, it is possible to calculate the target of the figure, i.e., the level that prices should reach in the phase following the breakout.

This is calculated by projecting, from the breaking point, the "base" of the triangle, i.e., the maximum width that the figure recorded during its formation.

The sixth figure in question concerns the formation of broadening.

Broadening

This represents a rather rare figure, classified as a variant of the triangle but which presents a contrary opening, with divergent trendlines. It is a figure that occurs at the end of a trend, usually bullish.

The dynamics of the volumes are different from that of the triangles, as the volume gradually expands together with the increase in price oscillation.

The seventh figure that we are going to examine concerns the diamond.

Diamond

Also, the diamond as an inversion figure is one of the rarest and one of the least simple to detect. Graphically the diamond is formed by a double-figure composed of a first half that recalls the shape of a broadening from a second half that resembles a symmetrical triangle.

A diamond can present itself in two circumstances:

1. at the end of an uptrend;
2. at the end of a bearish trend;

In the first case, it takes the name of "Diamond Top," and vice versa, we would be facing a "Diamond Bottom."

The figure does not always develop symmetrically. Often, the second half is prolonged in time more than the first one did.

By its nature, the diamond needs very dynamic market phases. The figure of the Diamond can also occur during simple breaks of the trend.

For this reason, it is easier to find the diamond at the peak of an upward trend before a bearish reversal rather than the other way around. The dynamics of volumes go hand in hand with that of prices. That is, if volumes increase, prices increase. In the second half, however, prices fall and consequently also volumes.

There are 4 basic elements to identify the training:

- an initial phase of price expansion;
- a maximum;
- a minimum;
- a phase of price contraction;

The pattern is only complete when the support or resistance line breaks and a pullback to the violated trendline do not always occur.

The minimum price target is equal to the maximum vertical distance between the two extreme parts of the figure projected at the bottom (or at the top) with respect to the breaking point of the support or resistance. It is possible, even for the diamond, to calculate a target price.

It is sufficient to project the maximum width of the figure and project it from the point where the breakout occurred.

If it is configured as a continuation figure, it is also possible to derive a second target, projecting the width of the movement that preceded the beginning of the diamond, from the point of the final breakout. diamond breaking points

The eighth figure we examine will be a figure difficult enough to examine and represents the rounding and spike.

Rounding and Spike

This represents one of the many figures of inversions, which presents itself as a slow and gradual movement on the lows that will first have a slight downward, then lateral and then shows a growing movement.

The pattern is one of the slowest of all the graphic analysis and is usually identifiable on longer-term charts.

It is really difficult to establish the precise moment in which the figure can be considered complete, if not after the first substantial rises. More difficult, it will be to identify upward targets.

Spike is also very special. The figures in question show, without any transition period, a sudden reversal of the quotations. An inversion accompanied by an explosion of volumes.

Due to its characteristics, the figure in question is difficult to identify in advance.

Double Top and Double Bottom

Also, this falls into the categories of the inversion figures, which we remember are particular graphic figures that announce an inversion of the current trend. The figure in question turns out to be a very common figure in graphic analysis and together with other figures, the double bottom and double top figures are among the most common and recognizable formations.

We explain briefly in two essential steps, its operation;

- **The double minimum is at the peak of a bearish trend and is configured as a minimum, a subsequent rebound and a subsequent fallback to the level of the previous minimum**. The ascent that follows leads to the completion of the figure. The pattern, due to its shape, is also called a formation in W. Volumes are growing during the formation of the first minimum, down in the following rebound, and then increase again during the upward movement that completes the figure.

Basically, therefore, the double minimum is realized, following a clear bearish trend, in which prices test twice a price threshold, but without being able to overcome it. This determines the realization of two minimums slightly spaced over time. Double minimum and double maximum.

1. Also, **the characteristics of the double maximum are the same, but the pattern has a secularly opposite**

development. The double top is at the height of an uptrend and is configured as a maximum, a consequent fall and a subsequent rebound towards the previous maximum.

The double maximum is achieved when, following a sharp uptrend, prices test twice a price threshold, but without being able to overcome it, determining the formation of two maximums. Volumes are growing at the formation of the first rise, remaining lower in the formation of the second maximum and then increasing conspicuously at the time of the piercing of the traceable line starting from the previous minimum.

In both figures, it is possible to observe a return of prices to the level of completion of the pattern, in a pullback similar to that of the head and shoulders that we will see later, before the definitive start of the new trend, bullish in the double minimum and bearish in the double maximum. This pullback is accompanied by small volumes.

The measurement of the minimum upward (or downward) target is calculated by calculating the distance between the line joining the two minima (or the two maxima) and the first maximum (or minimum) relative and projecting this value from the upward drilling point or downward.

in essence, the double minimum or the double maximum is, however, a graphic formation with a degree of reliability lower than other figures of inversion, both because it is not always detectable with sufficient certainty, and because it often occurs in conditions of volatility so high that allow identification of a valid breakout.

Triple Top and Triple Bottom

The triple maximum and the triple minimum are also inversion figures, defined as variants of the head and shoulders, but unlike the previous ones, the three maxima and the three minima are all placed at the same height.

The volumes to be considered, in the triple minimum correspond to each rise, starting from a minimum is accompanied by decreasing volumes. The pattern is completed when the line obtained by joining the last maximum with extremely high volumes is breached upwards. triple maximum

In the triple maximum, any downward correction starting from a maximum is accompanied by declining volumes, and consequently, the figure can be said to be complete, when the level obtained by joining the last lows is violated downwards with volumes in great growth. In the triple minimum, however, the minimum target is common to that used for head and shoulders (a figure that we will see shortly), if not also equal to the double minimum and double maximum, based on the height of the figure.

Chapter 9: Diversification and Managing Your Portfolio

How to diversify your investments? A good question that all investors ask themselves. After all, we must start from another question: why is it important to diversify your investments? Simple: to reduce risks. It goes without saying that investing in several different assets involves a better distribution of risk. So, if, for example, an action is at a loss, we will always have the hope that precious metal is on the rise instead.

Below we will try to offer a comprehensive picture on how to diversify your investments, thus better understanding why it is important to diversify your investments.

Why is it important to diversify? We have said that this practice is useful for reducing investment risks. The world today is globalized, so even the stock exchanges are extremely connected to each other. Therefore, the crisis of an exchange carries with it all the others. Furthermore, today's World, especially since the 1990s with the collapse of the Berlin

Wall, has become economically very variable and unpredictable. The logic that drives diversification responds to the impossibility of knowing in advance the future performance of our investments. A variable in which, substantially, the risk of each investment lies. The basic idea to minimize the risks deriving from this uncertainty consists in splitting its investments into different projects, thus spreading the risk linked to the performance of individual investments.

Moreover, each asset is linked to multiple variables. For example, actions are closely related to a company's performance. Which, often, also hides its real financial situation. Or agricultural raw materials, just a bacterium that destroys the crop to cause a collapse. Regarding the extraction of oil, just the disaster of a platform or a strike of the workers to cause the collapse of the flock. And what about a coup or unexpected election results.

How to diversify your investments? Before finding an answer, it is necessary to understand that investments are divided into 5 large areas:

- **Stock** - Area consisting of all shares, funds, ETFs, individual securities
- **Real estate** - This area includes financial instruments related to real estate
- **Commodities** - For commodities, we mean all those products mainly related to the soil, then cultivable. Like coffee, cocoa, sugar, soy, wheat. But also, to the subsoil, like the energy fields like oil, gas and so on.
- **Precious metals** - Precious metals include, as you can guess, gold, silver, platinum.
- **Bonds** - Bonds include both government securities and bonds issued by private companies.

Investing means making precise choices, selecting one asset rather than another. If I invest in share ownership, it means that I am deducting money from the other 4 markets.

However, it should always be kept in mind that money is something unfaithful. Because if today it is aimed at a type of investment, tomorrow it will move towards another. So, if today precious metals are good, tomorrow will sooner or later go to the raw materials. For tomorrow, obviously, we mean after a few years. So, it's like a few years' engagements. But when he changes partners, he ends up betraying billions of people who believed in that area of investment. And every time it's a severe blow because the values collapse

History is full of such betrayals. In 2007, for example, it happened to properties and shares. And the latter collapsed in 2000 as well. In 1980, however, it was the turn of gold. Of course, the stories of love are also prolonged, like that of the stock market started in 1984 and came up to 2000. Or like the one started in 2000 up to 2007 on real estate. Recently, however, money seems to have become attached to precious metals.

Therefore, money moves cyclically and even if it may happen that "fall in love" with more investment areas, it will do so more clearly towards an area. How to defend oneself from the volatility of the market? Surely inquire and train as much as possible, reading the economic news, taking a look at the countries on which to invest (considering their economic and political stability for example) or growing companies. Then it is advisable to rely on a trusted financial advisor to build your portfolio together.

What are the best assets to diversify your investments? Experts generally place MTB (acronym of multi-year Treasury Bonds) in the first place. Although the state coupons market is constantly evolving. In this historical moment, it is preferable to invest small amounts over the long term. However, it is worth stressing that these securities remain the safest investment to date, allowing a regular withdrawal of coupons with returns.

If we want faster and more substantial results, then the stock market is recommended for us. However, it must be said that large returns also correspond to much higher investment risks. So, we have to ponder perfectly how much to invest and on which institutions or companies. The properties are still to be avoided, since, after the bubble of the last decade, they have lost value. Although, it should also be added that the market believes that when the price falls, it is just the right time to buy. Just to get a regular monthly entry through rent. Or sell when the market is bullish again.

Bonds are another alternative, but it must be "guaranteed" and not subject to the performance of the companies to which they are affiliated. Finally, gold is always a good refuge, just like other precious materials or valuable paintings.

How to diversify our investments through the ETF? Many investors believe, naively, that it is enough to increase the number of investments to improve the diversification of the portfolio. But this is a dangerous simplification. If we invest our savings in individual securities, be they stocks or bonds, the number of products to be included in the portfolio must be raised to minimize the risk associated with each of the investments made.

On the other hand, if we invest our savings in active mutual funds or passive funds such as ETFs, we can achieve great diversification by reducing the number of instruments. Each fund (or ETF) is, in fact, a container of financial instruments, so with a few products, we can actually divide our portfolio into hundreds of different securities.

The main features of ETFs are:

- passive management
- their listing on the stock exchange as shares and bonds

With the former, it is intended that their return is closely linked to the listing of a stock exchange index and not to the fund manager's buying and selling ability. The stock index may be equity, commodity, bond, monetary, or other. The manager's job is limited to checking the consistency of the fund with the benchmark index. But also correct the value in the event of deviations. The difference between the price of the fund and that of the benchmark index is in the order of 1 or 2%.

"Passive management" therefore makes ETFs very cheap, to which is added their large or huge diversification, and their stock trading. All this makes them competitive compared to investing in individual stocks and less risky. However, there is also a lack of speculative lever leverage, inverted, or reversed leverage. ETFs are very convenient as they allow investing in many economic sectors: liquidity, bond indices, geographic equity markets, commodities, commodity sectors.

Example of diversification of investments

Suppose we have a capital to invest of 500 euros. And so, we decided to diversify investments in equal parts among the 5 assets. Now let's say that for each asset the trend was as follows:

Stocks: + 7%
Properties: - 6%
Commodities: - 10%
Precious metals: + 21%
Bonds: + 3%

Now, by making a calculation on the 100 euros invested per asset, we will have the following results: € 107 + € 94 + € 90 + € 121 + € 103 = € 515 total

We will, therefore, have earned € 15, or 3% on our initial invested capital. How is our result to be considered? It depends on our ambitions. If we play not to lose, then we will surely be satisfied. If we are traders who are content with little, we will be satisfied. If we do a more general calculation, perhaps considering an increase in personal expenses during the year, etc., then we will have a half reaction: we have not lost but not earned as well. If we are expert traders, then that 3% will appear miserable to us. Finally, if we are traders who want to push our earnings, then we will be completely dissatisfied. And we will think that perhaps having invested only in precious metals would have earned us 605 euros.

All this to say that the answer to the question of our satisfaction or not depends on us. From our ambitions. But of course, also from our formation. In fact, if we are beginners, then it is clear that for fear we will tend to distribute our money equally. But if we have the right experience and training on the subject, we will have the nose to invest in one or two assets only, those that we will consider being the winning ones.

Chapter 10: Swing Trading Options

Swing trading with options can be extremely difficult. This is why we decided to create this chapter, in which we go through some of the main ideas and concepts to always keep in mind, to be profitable from the start. Now, it is clear that at the beginning it is not easy to take money out of the market. However, with the right guidelines, it is not that difficult to achieve success in a short period of time. Anyway, let's get into some of the key factors to consider when it comes to swing trading with options.

1. *"If you are undecided, stay still."* It is not necessary to invest continuously. If you do not have precise ideas, it is better to do nothing and wait for clearer signs. Often times, the market is full of indecision: keep calm and stack up money for the future.

1. *"Cut losses and let profits run."* This is perhaps the best known and most important rule for those investing in the stock market. An indispensable factor for the application of this rule is the identification, immediately after the purchase, of the stop loss. This is how much you are willing to lose on that investment (consider when determining the average daily excursion of the stock). The cold and systematic application, even if painful, of the stop loss will preserve you from huge losses that would make the sale more and more traumatic, freezing capital that could be invested elsewhere.

1. *"Learn from your mistakes."* Errors are not always negative: if you follow a strategy with a method, if you apply the stop losses, you will not make particularly serious mistakes. Errors are an integral part of stock trading: you need to analyze why

you made them and what you can learn from them. In this way, a small loss can become a good investment lesson for the future.

1. *"Take profit and invest them back."* If one of our titles is on the rise, take profit will be applied as the stock grows. A stock cannot grow indefinitely, when the trend is reversed, selling at the top, we will have had a profit avoiding further descents. If then the title should go up again, it does not matter, it will go better next time. You cannot always sell at the top since you cannot time the market.

1. *"Buy on the rumor and sell on the news."* When positive news on a certain title officially comes out, pay attention. It may already be too late to invest in that title since the market could already have priced it in.

1. *Do not believe in "safe investments."* If someone tells you that a title will certainly reach a certain price, he either does not understand much of the stock market or is only doing his own interests.

1. *"Never become emotionally attached to a stock."* Some investors always follow a limited number of companies that they consider more reliable than others. There are no titles better than others, but only favorable situations and unfavorable situations. Often, instead of admitting an error, one perseveres on it with the consequence of being heavily unbalanced on a stock. This is really bad, especially if you are overcommitted to a stock in which, at that moment, the market does not believe in.

1. *"Always maintain certain liquidity available."* Cyclically we

find ourselves in situations of several days of generalized decline of the whole stock exchange and often, for lack of liquidity, we cannot grasp excellent buying opportunities. Keep some money aside to jump on big opportunities.

1. *"Choose the right platform."* One important rule for investing in the stock market is that the platform makes a difference. Carefully selecting safe, honest and reliable trading platforms is the first step to make money. Those who start investing in the stock market for the first time must be careful to choose platforms that are really simple to use, perhaps with high-quality educational support. Some platforms also offer add-on tools, such as notifications, social trading and free analysis tools to guide less experienced traders.

1. *"Invest only in what you understand."* As the "guru" of finance Warren Buffett said, "never, never, invest in something that you do not understand, and above all, that you do not know." The overwhelming majority of investors can achieve their capital growth goals by using the most common financial instruments, which are almost always simple to understand. The complex tools are best left to the great experts in the field.

1. *"Diversify your portfolio."* When investing, the word to keep in mind is "diversification." Never invest in a single title, because if that sinks, your money will come to the same end. It is always better to have diversified investments to minimize the specific risks of a company, a market, an asset class or a currency. The more you diversify and the lower the probability of having drastic falls.

1. *"Understand and evaluate the risk."* The risk is an intrinsic component of every investment. If it does not exist, there is no

return. Whether they are government bonds, stocks or mutual funds, they all have a risk component, which will obviously be greater if you want to hope for higher returns. So, if someone tells you that there is an investment without risk, it means that it is better to get advice from someone else.

1. *"Look beyond direct investment."* As an alternative to direct purchase of shares, it is possible to invest in the stock market indexes, through ETFs (listed mutual funds, which replicate the performance of equity and bond indices), or in mutual funds, that offer a high diversification even with minimum amounts, allow you to invest small periodic shares, for example 100 euros per month, and may even provide a monthly coupon.

1. *"Do not follow the masses."* The typical decision of who buys stocks by investing in the stock market is usually strongly influenced by the advice of acquaintances, neighbors, or relatives. So, if everyone around is investing in a particular company, a beginner investor tends to do the same. But this strategy is bound to fail in the long run, and it is not the right approach. There should be no need to say that you should always avoid having a herd mentality if you do not want to lose hard-earned money on the stock market. The world's biggest investor, Warren Buffett, is right when he says, "Be fearful when others are greedy, and be greedy when others are fearful!"

1. *"Do not try to time the market."* One thing that Warren Buffett does not do is try to time the stock market, even if he has a very strong understanding of the key price levels of the single shares. Most investors, however, do exactly the opposite, which often causes losses of money. So, you should never try

to give timing to the market a chance. In reality, no one has ever succeeded in doing so successfully and consistently over multiple market cycles.

1. ***"Be disciplined."*** Historically, it has often happened that during periods of a high market upswing, we first caused moments of panic. Market volatility has inevitably made investors poorer, even if the market moved in the intended direction. Therefore, it is prudent to have patience and follow a disciplined investment approach as well as keeping a long-term general picture in mind.

1. ***"Be realistic and do not hope."*** There is nothing wrong with hoping to make the best investment, but you could be in trouble if the financial goals are not based on realistic assumptions. For example, many stocks have generated more than 50 percent of returns during the big uptrend in recent years. However, this does not mean that we can always expect the same kind of return from the stock exchange.

1. ***"Keep your portfolio under control."*** We live in a connected world. Every important event that happens anywhere in the world also has an impact on our money. So, we have to monitor our portfolio and make adjustments constantly.

1. ***"Be sure to be on the legal side of things."*** If someone proposes an investment, it must be verified as an "authorized project." In our country, those who offer financial investments must be authorized by law, and this is an important safeguard for savers. In fact, the authorization is issued only in the presence of the requested requisites and, once authorized, the financial intermediaries are subject to constant supervision. Checking this is not particularly demanding: if you have internet you

can even directly access the information held by the supervisory authorities; otherwise you can contact the authorities themselves using traditional means.

1. **"Be skeptical and do your own research."** Nobody gives anything for nothing: be wary of investment proposals that ensure a very high return. At the promise of high returns, there are usually very high risks or, in some cases, even attempts of fraud. Be wary of the "Ponzi schemes." These "operations," in fact, cannot guarantee any kind of return, as they are normally supplied exclusively by the continuity of the accessions. In other words, when the new signatures are no longer sufficient to pay the "interests" to the previous subscribers, the schemes are destined to fail. Be wary of the vague and generic investment proposals, for which the methods for using the money collected are not explained in detail (what kind of securities will be purchased, at what prices, on which markets, with which risk profiles - interest rate, foreign exchange or counterparty - and whether and which hedging instruments will be used to cover such risks).

1. **"Have a long-term mindset."** According to Warren Buffett, the shares once bought, are not to be sold. It is, therefore, better to evaluate the industrial trends in the long term and then buy them, leaving aside the passengers' enthusiasm.

1. **"When investing in real estate, know the area you are investing in."** To start with, it is good that you put your focus on your area of residence or, if you live in a big city, even on your neighborhood or on one that you know well. If you think to act on a field of action too large, you risk dispersing too much energy towards something that can present totally different solutions. Dedicate yourself only to residential

buildings, apartments or houses. The commercial ones, even if they can be very profitable, have other rules and in general greater difficulties. The same for the land: you can do big business, but it is not something suitable for those who start.

1. *"Choose the right leverage and use it to your advantage."* Real estate investments must be done with leverage. If you want to make an investment only with your money, then the essence of real estate investment is not clear to you. In fact, the concept of financial leverage allows you to invest with money that is not yours but to make money directly for you. Leverage an economic tool that allows you to get where you would not get only with your own strength. You can take out a mortgage (if you can afford it) or engage financial partners. It may seem strange to you, but it is not at all: even the richest need partners and remember that a figure that seems almost unimaginable to you, it may be normal to somebody else.

1. "*Verba volant, scripta manent*" the Latins used to say. So never make verbal agreements, even if it is a relative or a childhood friend. Consult a lawyer to have the templates of the documents to be used. Like everything, at first it will seem difficult, but after a few times you will become an expert in basic legal practices for the sale of real estate, and you will be able to create documents in a very short time even by yourself.

1. *"Consider shorter positions."* In the fixed income universe, a short duration approach is potentially able to reduce sensitivity to rising interest rates, while optimizing the returns/risk rations

1. *"Know your risk/reward ratio."* A higher return may be tempting, but you must be sure not to take too many risks

about the remuneration you would get. In bond markets, this means avoiding lengthening duration in a context of rising interest rates. Increasing investments in riskier assets may seem appropriate at the moment (when the macroeconomic scenario is quite positive), but it could turn out to be a rather risky choice if the situation should change. For example, the yields offered by high yield debt, on average 3% in Europe and 5.5% in the United States, would not be sufficient to compensate investors if insolvencies passed from their current level of 2% to a more normal one of the 5%. Conversely, market areas with a good risk/return profile, with high-rated issuers offering attractive returns, include emerging market debt, subordinated financial bonds, and hybrid corporate bonds. Aiming at long-term quality makes it possible to take on fair risks, helping to limit the impact of any negative macroeconomic event.

1. *"Take the currency pairing into account."* Global investments are exposed to currency risks. High yield bonds and emerging market funds, for example, are usually denominated in US dollars, but the underlying bonds they hold may be issued in another currency. Fund managers may choose to include currency risk in the overall portfolio risk as exchange rates fluctuate or decide to contain this risk through currency hedging.

1. *"Stay flexible, keep some cash aside."* It is important to have the flexibility to underwrite and liquidate investments to seize the best opportunities. However, trades are expensive and can quickly erode earnings. This happens above all in the bond markets, given the relatively low levels of returns. The bid-ask spread is on average 30-40% of the yield, so an excess of trades erodes this margin and obviously reduces the total return.

Even holding portfolios with structurally short duration, allowing short-term bonds to come to maturity naturally, can improve returns because you will effectively pay the bid-ask spread once.

1. **"Build up your portfolio over time."** If investing a small sum such as 5000 Euro, will not allow you to live on that income, it can certainly represent an opportunity, to make money. Also, even if you have good economic availability, the ideal is always "to make it safe," start to invest from small figures and then fuel the investment over time.

1. **"*The past does not equal the future.*"** The story is not indicative of how an investment will result in the future and investors should always try to weigh the potential risks associated with a particular investment, as well as its possible returns.

Once you have established a profitable options trading strategy that generates a passive income every single month, you cannot fly to Thailand and live the laptop lifestyle just yet. As the millionaire Tony Robbins said, *just because it works, it does not mean it will last forever*. I really want this to sink in as it is one of the most important notions of the entire book.

When things are moving in the right direction, it is time to triple down on your effort and truly commit yourself to mastery. In particular, there is one thing that I'd like you to do once the first profits start to come.

Find a mentor

One of the great things about success is that it leaves footsteps: almost anything you would like to do to improve your life has already been done by someone else. It does not matter whether you are starting a business, beginning your trading journey, having a happy marriage, losing weight, quitting smoking, running a marathon or simply organizing a perfect lunch. There is certainly someone who did it very well and has left some clues.

When you are able to take advantage of these precious clues, you will discover that life is like a game in which you must connect the dots, and all the dots have already been identified and organized by others. All you have to do is follow their project and use their system.

Chapter 11: Things to Ponder Before Entering the Market

In this chapter, we will go deep into the subject and discover the 15 golden lessons that every investor should know, before entering the stock market.

Easy Money is Like Santa Claus: "It does not exist!"

One who promises to quintuple your assets without sweating is not more than a seller of smoke. Investing in the stock market is not a joke. To achieve the investment goals, you have set yourself to avoid risky securities, focus on something more stable, lasting, and profitable. In the recipe for success, in addition to a serious knowledge of the stock markets, there is also the sentimental component (for those investing there is no room for panic but a lot of patience) and even a bit of luck.

Gold and Cash do not Give Interest

Everyone knows that cash does not disappear, but after the bizarre maneuvers of the European Central Bank (which brought negative returns on the single currency), we can be even more certain that investing in cash does not create any interest. The dream of all is to be able to accumulate that amount of money enough to enjoy a quiet retirement but the closer it gets to the time x, the more the small investor tends to panic. Hence the reckless choices to invest in cash or in commodities such as gold which, although it proves to be more stable than fiat, cannot hold the same value forever. Just think that in the last luster, the value of the most precious metal fell by 34.8%.

The Recipe for a Winning Strategy

One of the main factors of success on the stock exchange is sentiment: patience, foresight, and prudence are the three basic ingredients of winning strategies, but it is also true that a little risk never hurts.

If the money we have invested on a certain stock does not return, you should look around and find some slightly riskier but at least profitable activity, with the hope that an important injection of money into the markets can restart the economy by stimulating productivity and development.

Establish Investment Goals

Before starting to invest, then embark on a challenging and long path, you must have clear in mind where you want to go. It depends on personal aspirations, on the trust that one has for himself and on many other factors. However, the main choice is between protecting capital and making it grow. Under certain conditions, the stock exchange also lends itself to the speculative approach. Who wants to start could also establish concrete objectives such as buying a good or a service. In any case, the rule is always the same: to understand where you want to arrive.

Establish the Degree of Risk Tolerance

This is probably the most important phase. The stock market is in fact extremely varied and allows numerous approaches, from the prudent and static to the dynamic and courageous.

This is why it is always good to establish one's degree of tolerance. Based on this decision, further choices will be made, until the real investment is realized. Investor profiles depend on personal characteristics and their economic situation. If you are a simple worker, do not sail in gold and maybe those who invest are the savings of a lifetime, it is good to give up any speculative ambitions. The degree of tolerance determines the risk that you intend to run and the strategy that will be adopted later.

Studying

The information issue should not be forgotten. The stock market is complex, structurally risky, so we need to be cautious. The risk is to lose capital in a short period. Therefore, it is necessary to undertake a training course that confers at least the theoretical tools. The topic of the study should consist of both the investment modalities - how it is invested in the concrete - and the economic environment in general.

As for the sources, including paper texts, successful books, and the internet, you are spoiled
with choices.

The study activity, however, never abandons the investor, even when he has become an expert. Pressing is the need to update continuously, but also to inquire about everything that gravitates around the securities in the portfolio.

Choose the Long Term

Investing in the stock market should not be an activity of a few months or even a few years. It must be a continuous activity. It is only through patience and perseverance that it is possible to make substantial profits. This means that you need to build a long-term version (which looks at least for the next five years [ten is more suitable]). This means that it is okay not to give in to the temptation to sell the securities as soon as the prices start to fall. Life is worth the saying, "laugh well who laughs last."

Monitoring

If you opt for a long-term vision, as you should, then it is essential to monitor the status of your investment. Not everyone knows that control and monitoring begin before the investment itself. In particular, it is necessary to establish a benchmark, i.e., a yardstick by means of which it is possible to really understand whether we are on the right path or not. Finally, it is good to make a periodic comparison between the expected results and the real ones. In the beginning, there is a strong temptation to abandon oneself to discouragement, also because the results tend to arrive farther with time.

A general consideration can be made on the segment within which to operate. In fact, everything depends on risk tolerance. If this is very low, you should address those segments that by their nature do not suffer from the crisis. The reference is to those goods whose consumption is practically mandatory, therefore the food and pharmaceuticals. Investing in pharmaceutical companies' actions will not make you rich but is a very useful asset to protect capital. Strangely enough, but up to a certain point, the high-tech segment (e.g., mobile phones, social networks, etc.) also plays a similar role.

Investing in the stock market can be a business that can increase its capital. In addition to technical knowledge, we need some moral skills: patience, perseverance, lucidity, foresight. All qualities that must be cultivated and that can make the difference. Vice versa will never give good fruits an approach based on imprudence, on haste, from the frenzy of profit.

Use the Leverage

What unfortunately many traders do not consider is investing in the stock market or trading online using leverage. To invest in the stock market with little money, it is necessary to deepen the study of this tool, which will allow us to expose our capital to a huge risk. We recommend the use of leverage only on a reduced capital, carried out concurrently also with a rationalized use of stop loss and take profit. Besides, you must always have your budget under control using careful Money Management. Finally, before investing in the stock market, you need to study the markets and all the financial instruments on which you want to invest in.

"You do not need to be a finance guru to invest in the stock market!"

Obviously, we are not telling you that the market should not be studied or that there must be a basis for training. One who applies himself and follows the markets, deepening the subject, will always know more than others.

So, we always recommend following the training path of your broker, which will allow you not to take missteps throughout the investment process. Through taking advantage of the online trading demo platforms, it is possible to simulate the investment and understand where mistakes are made and avoid them when investing with a real account.

Conclusion

Thank you and congratulations for making it through to the end of *"Options Trading."* Let's hope that it was informative and able to provide you with all of the tools you need to achieve your financial goals.

The next step is to begin applying what you have learned during this book. Our suggestion is always to open up a demo account on a broker and make a few tries before putting real money into it. Remember that you should never risk more than what you can afford to lose; so manage your capital wisely.

We hope that you find these lessons valuable and that you got the information you were looking for. Letting your money work for you will give you an incredible feeling, especially at the beginning when you make the first gains. We are thrilled for you to start, and we cannot wait to see your results coming in!

© Copyright 2019_All rights reserved.

The following eBook is reproduced below with the goal of providing information that is as accurate and reliable as possible. Regardless, purchasing this eBook can be seen as consent to the fact that both the publisher and the author of this book are in no way experts on the topics discussed within and that any recommendations or suggestions that are made herein are for entertainment purposes only. Professionals should be consulted as needed prior to undertaking any of the action endorsed herein.

This declaration is deemed fair and valid by both the American Bar Association and the Committee of Publishers Association and is legally binding throughout the United States.

Furthermore, the transmission, duplication, or reproduction of any of the following work including specific information will be considered an illegal act irrespective of if it is done electronically or in print. This extends to creating a secondary or tertiary copy of the work or a recorded copy and is only allowed with the express written consent from the Publisher. All additional right reserved.

The information in the following pages is broadly considered a truthful and accurate account of facts and as such, any inattention, use, or misuse of the information in question by the reader will render any resulting actions solely under their purview. There are no scenarios in which the publisher or the original author of this work can be in any fashion deemed liable for any hardship or damages that may befall them after undertaking information described herein.

Additionally, the information in the following pages is intended only for informational purposes and should thus be thought of as universal. As befitting its nature, it is presented without assurance regarding its prolonged validity or interim quality. Trademarks that are mentioned are done without written consent and can in no way be considered an endorsement from the trademark holder